"I have known Cynthia Spell Humbert and her excellent therapeutic skills for many years. I am very thankful that she wrote this extremely helpful and timely book. We are living in an addiction-prone society and addictions are caused by shame and lack of connectedness."

—PAUL MEIER, M.D.,
psychiatrist, co-founder of New Life Clinics

"Bravo to Cynthia Spell Humbert! *Deceived by Shame, Desired by God* is a unique blending of deep theological truth and psychological insights. With a warm story-telling style, Cynthia has crafted a gift for all who desire for God to rent the veil of shame that separates them from full experience of His presence. The small-group study guide is an added bonus."

—GARY W. MOON, PH.D.,
professor and vice president, Psychological Studies Institute,
director of research and development, LifeSprings Resources,
author of The Bible Ride series

Deceived by Shame, Desired by God

INCLUDES A TWELVE-WEEK BIBLE STUDY

WOMEN OF WISDOM SERIES

Cynthia Spell Humbert

NAVPRESS

BRINGING TRUTH TO LIFE
P.O. Box 35001, Colorado Springs, Colorado 80935

OUR GUARANTEE TO YOU

We believe so strongly in the message of our books that
we are making this quality guarantee to you. If for any
reason you are disappointed with the content of this
book, return the title page to us with your name and
address and we will refund to you the list price of the
book. To help us serve you better, please briefly describe
why you were disappointed. Mail your refund request to:
NavPress, P.O. Box 35002, Colorado Springs, CO 80935.

The Navigators is an international Christian organization. Our mission is to reach, disciple,
and equip people to know Christ and to make Him known through successive generations. We
envision multitudes of diverse people in the United States and every other nation who have
a passionate love for Christ, live a lifestyle of sharing Christ's love, and multiply spiritual
laborers among those without Christ.

NavPress is the publishing ministry of The Navigators. NavPress publications help believers
learn biblical truth and apply what they learn to their lives and ministries. Our mission is to
stimulate spiritual formation among our readers.

Library of Congress Catalog Card Number: 2001030165
ISBN 1-57683-219-8

Cover design by Dan Jamison
Cover photo by Peter Johansky/FPG
Creative Team: Pam Mellskog, Lori Mitchell, Glynese Northam

Some of the anecdotal illustrations in this book are true to life and are included with the permission of the persons involved. All other illustrations are composites of real situations, and
any resemblance to people living or dead is coincidental.

Unless otherwise identified, all Scripture quotations in this publication are taken from the HOLY
BIBLE: NEW INTERNATIONAL VERSION® (NIV®). Copyright © 1973, 1978, 1984 by
International Bible Society. Used by permission of Zondervan Publishing House. All rights
reserved. Other versions used include: The Message: New Testament with Psalms and Proverbs
(MSG) by Eugene H. Peterson, copyright © 1993, 1994, 1995, used by permission of NavPress
Publishing Group; the New American Standard Bible (NASB), © The Lockman Foundation
1960, 1962, 1963, 1968, 1971, 1972, 1973, 1975, 1977; the New Revised Standard Version
(NRSV), copyright © 1989, by the Division of Christian Education of the National Council of
the Churches of Christ in the USA, used by permission, all rights reserved; and the New King
James Version (NKJV), copyright © 1979, 1980, 1982, 1990, Thomas Nelson Inc., Publishers.

Humbert, Cynthia.
    Deceived by shame, desired by God / Cynthia Spell Humbert.
      p. cm. 00 (Women of wisdom series)
    Includes bibliographical references.
    ISBN 1-57683-219-8
    1. Shame--Religious aspects--Christianity. 2. Christian women--Religious life. I. Title.
II. Series.

BT714.H86 2001
248.8'43--DC21   2001030165

Printed in the United States of America

1 2 3 4 5 6 7 8 9 10 / 05 04 03 02 01

FOR A FREE CATALOG OF
NAVPRESS BOOKS & BIBLE STUDIES,
CALL 1-800-366-7788 (USA)
OR 1-416-499-4615 (CANADA)

Dedication

*This book is dedicated with great love
to my husband David.
Thank you for being the most unselfish
person I have ever known.*

*And to my children — Elisabeth, Christian,
and Mary Camille — you bring
my heart great joy!*

Table of Contents

Foreword

If you enjoy being miserable, don't read this book. However, if you long for transformation to a life that offers joy, completeness, peace, forgiveness, personal worth, and healing, start reading immediately! There has never been a time in history when the message of this book has been more urgently needed. Every week I meet women who have been deceived by the lies of the Enemy due to the abuse of the past, the addictions of the present, the shame of wrong choices, the imperfections of the body, or by the crushing of the spirit.

All women have expectations that dissolve into disappointment. We get disappointed when what we expected in a relationship or an experience falls short of what we received, or when we make a choice that catapults us into hidden, shameful places. Those disappointments promote a longing for change. We often respond with emotions that are based on our personalities and past experiences. Some are "hot reactors;" others are "slow boilers;" and others, due to the hurts of the past "stuff and deny" their emotions. At that point we run our emotions through the grid of our belief system and choose a response that results in an action that either embraces God's love or a response that compounds our shame due to the deception of the Enemy.

Cynthia Spell Humbert's credentials and experience as a Christian therapist have given her the background and wisdom to write a book that addresses the needs of today's woman. *Deceived by Shame, Desired by God* is filled with encouragement, biblical wisdom, and case studies that women can understand. Whether you are a woman living the shame of wrong choices or with the victimization of the past, you will find a road to hope and healing in this well-written book. If you work with women who are dealing with past and present issues, this book will be a welcome addition to your ministry tools. The Bible study included in the book gives added value to the Christian leader who wants to assist others in their journey to wholeness. This book will grab your heart and grip your soul.

Not only is Cynthia a gifted writer, she is a skilled professional Christian speaker. With intelligence, Southern charm, grace, humor, and vulnerability, Cynthia communicates in dynamic, inspiring. and practical ways. Her solid foundation in biblical truth offers listeners and readers hope, help, and healing love. This book will free women who have been plagued by shame to recognize their worth, embrace God's grace, and begin building a heritage that leads to a positive and productive future. I highly recommend it!

—Carol Kent, President
Speak Up Speaker Services and
Author, *Becoming a Woman of Influence* (NavPress)

Acknowledgments

I am deeply grateful to the many people who have prayed for me and supported me during the writing of this book. As I wrote this book, I was expecting our third child, and the going wasn't always easy. As a matter of fact, I was known to moan and groan on a daily basis! Many thanks to those dear people who helped care for my children and lifted me up in special ways during the stressful months of trying to deliver the book before I delivered the baby!

I am forever indebted to all of the clients who have trusted me with their stories and their hearts throughout my years as a counselor. Without you, this book would not be possible. You have taught me many lessons about life and God's ability to change us each by His compassion, love, and grace. I am enriched by your courage and wisdom. Your lessons will now be used by God to bless the hearts of many.

This book would never have started without the encouragement of Carol Kent. Thank you for pushing me a little and for opening the doors to make this dream of mine come true. You are a special friend and a wonderful woman of God!

To the NavPress publishing team. . ."WOW!" I had no idea how much God would use you all to bless me! Jan Maniatis, thanks for believing in this project from the start! The gift of your friendship is icing on the cake! Nanci McAlister, you are a wonderful encourager! Pam Mellskog, thanks for cleaning up this manuscript with your editorial knowledge. You all know how to make your authors feel valued!

I could never write and teach without my husband David's incredible support and encouragement. Your patience is greatly appreciated as well as your ability to "not sweat the small stuff!" Thanks for cheering me on to the finish line of this project! I love you dearly.

Elisabeth, Christian, and Mary Camille, you are the greatest blessings in the world! Thanks for teaching Mommy about the simple joys of life and for reminding me daily of God's unconditional love and grace for all of His children. I am forever enriched by your lives and your love!

Mother, you are the best! Thank you for being my lifelong cheerleader and for always telling me I could do anything Jesus called me to do. You are often the glue that holds me together!

Special gratitude to Jane, Nita, Donna, Pat, Heather, and all of the brave women who were willing to be vulnerable with their stories in order to help others. Be encouraged to know that God is not "wasting your valleys," but is using them now to comfort others. Patty VanCleave, thanks for your daily prayers and helpful insights into the Bible study!

To all those who have touched my life in significant ways, your names may not be mentioned in this book, but you know who you are, and I thank you.

My greatest appreciation goes to my Lord and Savior Jesus Christ who has "redeemed my life from the pit and crowns me with love and compassion" (Psalm 103:4). I am overwhelmed with wonder that You daily give me that which I don't deserve—Your matchless gift of grace!

Part I:

―❦―

The Many Reflections
of Shame

―❦―

one

THE GREATEST DECEPTION: ENOUGH SHAME TO COVER EVERYONE

Let us fix our eyes on Jesus, the author and perfecter
of our faith, who for the joy set before him endured
the cross, scorning its shame, and sat down
at the right hand of the throne of God.
Consider him who endured such opposition from sinful
men, so that you will not grow weary and lose heart.
HEBREWS 12:2-3

"I have ruined everything!" Catherine shouted through her tears. "Just look at my child! I don't even know who her father is! How will I ever explain that to her? God could never forgive me for being such a failure!" The forlorn twenty-two-year-old woman clutched her newborn baby and rocked back and forth on the sofa, inconsolable.

Mothers usually don't bring their children along to counseling sessions. So it surprised me when Catherine introduced herself in the waiting room earlier that morning with her infant in tow. The moment we met, she began apologizing profusely, explaining that she couldn't find a sitter and had no family in town to help her with emergency child care.

It turns out that this new client felt apologetic about a whole lot more than that. Through many emotionally charged sessions, I began understanding the vast stores of hurt, anger, and damage she had tucked away in her heart—the specific reasons why she felt regretful and depressed so much of the time.

First of all, she had grown up as a pastor's daughter and felt like she lived in a fish bowl. Somehow people only saw a perfect family behind the glass—not the one terrorized by a controlling, manipulative man who batted her and her brother around if their rooms fell out of perfect order. Other times, her father needed no excuse to shove them into the walls or hit them with his fist or his belt in places where others couldn't see the marks. When her mother tried to protect the children from his wrath, he would turn on her too.

After discussing the troubled relationship with her father session after session, I finally encouraged her to discuss how her mother treated her. "Tenderly," she had softly answered. And as an adult, it saddened Catherine to realize how dependent and fearful her mother must have been of this tyrant.

"My mother was the only calming factor in my early life," Catherine sniffled. "She held us a lot and prayed with us. I remember her encouraging me to put my faith and trust in God. So, I viewed my relationship with God as my life raft in the sea of pain and confusion caused by my father. I found a sweet security knowing that God loved me uniquely and cared about my feelings." The distraught young woman paused a moment and then sobbed so energetically that it choked the rest of her words for several minutes.

Though Catherine continued maturing in her faith as a teen by reading the Bible daily and devouring as many books regarding Christianity as she could get her hands on, her past caught up with her in college. At that point, she fell into a severe depression from so many years of stuffing her feelings.

Why would God allow her father to continually taunt and abuse her and the rest of the family while he claimed to be a godly man? Her anger and confusion mounted the more she thought about his hidden alter ego. His on-the-job life of preaching on Sundays and faithfully ministering to the congregation throughout the week made a perfect foil to his at-home behavior. There, he only mentioned God to manipulate her. If, for instance, she did not do things perfectly and obey his demands, he threatened that God would no longer love her.

Instead of seeking therapy at that point, she began numbing her pain with alcohol and casual sexual relationships.

"But I sobered up pretty quickly when I missed my period," she explained as tears streamed down her cheeks. "I had been with two different men that month, and I don't know which one is the father. It doesn't really matter. They aren't the kind of guys who would care about helping with a baby. I mentioned the pregnancy to one of them, and he laughed and told me it probably wasn't his, and that since I was such a slut, I should go to the nearest abortion clinic. At least I didn't have an abortion. I knew two wrongs couldn't make one right, and that I had to keep the baby."

Looking down at her sleeping daughter, she wondered aloud if God could ever love her again. Would anyone want to marry someone like her? And why, oh why, did she walk away from God and make such bad choices?

Consequences of Sin

Unfortunately, Catherine's not the only one to lament like this. In a split-second of disobedience, Adam and Eve suffered immediate negative consequences, and they and everyone else have been suffering ever since. The brokenness I see every day stems from this original sin. In Adam and Eve's case, the consequences of sin caused them to:

☞ Feel ashamed of their nakedness and try to cover up.
☞ Open the world to sin and death, destroying paradise.

🌱 Sever their formerly unhampered connection to God and to eternal life.

🌱 Fear God and hide from Him.

🌱 Reject God's attempt at restoring fellowship because they doubted His ability to forgive them for their disobedience.

🌱 Prompt God to set into motion a plan of grace and redemption.

In *The Gift to All People,* Max Lucado reflects on the consequences of original sin: "The moment the forbidden fruit touched the lips of Eve, the shadow of a cross appeared on the horizon. And between that moment and the moment the man with the mallet placed the spike against the wrist of God, a master plan was fulfilled."

It's important to understand that sin always involves a choice. And no matter what sin you choose, it will be like every other sin across the span of human history in that it involves disobeying God.

Willingness to Willfulness

Never allow anyone to fool you with the idea that the "New Age Movement" is somehow "new." The very premise of this false religion is that we are all connected to a universal power, and eventually—with enough "self-awareness"—we can seize power and become our own god. But you don't have to read many chapters in Genesis to see that "seizing power" is the original deception Satan used to score in the Garden.

In those early days of Eden, Adam and Eve had a willingness to obey God and to trust Him with their whole hearts. This produced a tender relationship with the Creator God, one filled with love, security, joy, and peace. Open, honest, and safe communication defined this perfect relationship. They understood and accepted the gift of eternal life, knowing that it meant endless communion with the Father-God who loved to laugh and play with them, who delighted in watching His dear children enjoy His creation.

Then came that horrible day when man made a choice to willfully disobey. As certainly as slitting one's own throat separates a person from the flow of life, so original sin severed our relationship with God and introduced sin and spiritual death. Ever since, we have felt ashamed, out of control, alone, isolated, and afraid of abandonment.

At the very depth of our soul, we have felt a longing for restored relationship, but the lie says we can never be good enough, never work hard enough to earn and regain the love of God. But thanks be to God that by His immeasurable grace (and other riches we do not deserve and could never earn), He leads us on a journey of restoration, back into a place of willingness to rest in His love and allow Him to be in control.

In *Homesick for Eden*, Gary Moon asserts, "Few would argue against the notion that the most important choice humans are faced with is the choice between willingness and willfulness—between surrender to a reality greater than oneself and self-sufficiency."

Just Call Me Eve

When I experience the moodiness and cramping associated with PMS or the slow final months of pregnancy when every day seems to last a week, I joke with friends about Eve. Since this is all her fault, I plan to be the first one in heaven to line up and slap her cross-eyed for the curse that her disobedience brought on all women.

Other times, in humility, I admit that my name might as well be Eve. If I had been in the Garden of Eden, I would have gotten to the Tree of the Knowledge of Good and Evil much faster than she did. I would have raced there as fast as I could just to look at the forbidden fruit, just to touch it for a moment . . . just to hold it in my hand. Then, I would have probably wanted a tiny bite—just a small taste of what God forbids. But you don't have to be in the Garden to realize that seemingly small sins can create huge chasms between you and God.

Today, God still draws a line in the sand for us and then tells us to avoid crossing the line in order to avoid getting hurt. But, like rebellious children, we pace back and forth parallel to the line—each time walking a little bit closer trying to see how close we can get without crossing it. Finally, in defiance, we put a big toe over the line. We wishfully think that we can cross over just a little and nothing bad will happen. But, as far as God's concerned, one big toe over the line might as well be a full body flop over it. Why? Partial disobedience is total disobedience.

Like Eve, people who cross over God's line by sinning often see the gulf between themselves and God get as wide as the Grand Canyon. Eventually, the person who sinned may feel alone and hopeless—completely aware that there's no way to reconnect or reestablish a relationship with God without confessing, repenting, and accepting forgiveness.

Some consequences, such as being arrested for driving while intoxicated, being picked up for shoplifting, admitting to an out-of-wedlock pregnancy, gaining weight due to compulsive overeating, or going through a divorce due to an adulterous affair, are experienced with a shameful awareness of public and external consequences. But the consequences of sin are not always external or visible to others. For instance, it's relatively easy to hide sins like sexual promiscuity, an abortion, bulimia or anorexia, hatred, and bitterness.

But both types of sin cause separation from God and can produce the same amount of shame. This shame causes loneliness, fear, and a profound emptiness. Often, a shame-filled person knows that she somehow needs to find a way back home, but many choose the wrong paths for the journey—roads that lead away from God and deeper into self-abusive behaviors, which only make feelings of shame more pronounced.

Understanding Shame

Shame is a paralyzing emotion in which the afflicted person believes irreparable damage has been done to the deepest part of her soul. Shame may not necessarily originate from a behavior perceived as shameful. Rather, sufferers describe this feeling as an internal wound so painful and heavy that it makes them feel flawed for even existing.

Before Adam and Eve disobeyed God, "they were naked and not ashamed" (Genesis 2:25). In this case, Adam and Eve's unabashed nakedness conveyed their sense of being totally open and exposed before God. Nakedness symbolized their authentic and true selves. They lived a life of complete honesty with each other and with God. There was nothing to hide— they easily accepted themselves and felt no shame.

However, immediately after they sinned, they ran to hide from God because they knew they were now naked and exposed. They immediately felt a deep sense of shame. Shame is a lie from Satan because it involves a deeply felt perception of permanent unacceptability—to God, to others, and to self. That explains why shame pushes people to hide their true selves. They fear that if you see the real them, you will be appalled and reject them.

Consequently, those struggling with shame spend lots of time and energy creating a "cover-up" to hide it from God and others. They hope that in this way their sin and brokenness will go unnoticed. But shame is like an internal weed with far reaching roots that strangle healthy thinking, emotions, and actions.

In *Healing the Shame That Binds You*, John Bradshaw explores different levels of shame including the most serious, toxic, life-destroying shame. Toxic shame involves an excruciatingly internal experience of unexpected and unwanted exposure. It is a deep cut felt primarily from the inside. It divides you from yourself and from others. Why? In this case, you disown yourself, and this disowning demands a cover-up. Toxic shame loves darkness and secretiveness.

Shame always produces shame. If parents or caregivers are filled with it, they will pass some degree of it along to the next generation. For instance, you may learn to feel shame about who you are when a parent or caregiver neglects or abuses you—emotionally, verbally, spiritually, physically, or sexually. Furthermore, caregivers who are actively trapped in addictions have no emotional inheritance to offer their children except a legacy of hopelessness and shame. But you can feel shamed by relatives, your peer group, society, and even your church as well.

No wonder shame makes people afraid of intimate relationships. There is a deep fear that if you find out how messed up I really am, you will abandon me. Those struggling with shame often view others as "normal," acceptable, and lovable. Yet, they see themselves as flawed, damaged, and different. It becomes as natural as breathing for them to shame themselves with critical self-talk. Ultimately, shame creates a feeling of being lost and confused, not knowing what you feel or how to communicate with others. It is impossible to let someone else know you if you don't even know yourself. So, the shame-driven person uses even more energy to cover up and keep secrets by assuming a role—that of the false self. It takes so much energy to keep hiding that there's scarcely energy left for anything else. Too often, this hiding from yourself and others causes great loneliness and suffering.

Walking Through Shame

Lisa could hardly remember a time when she did not feel ashamed. In fact, one of her earliest memories was of her first grade teacher pulling her aside and telling her not to come back to class "in those same filthy clothes." Humiliated and crushed, Lisa pretended that no one overheard in order to cope with the comment. But at age six, she already knew the shame and desperation of her situation—she didn't need the teacher's reminder. Her parents were divorced, and her mother was a raging alcoholic who had no time for her children. There was rarely enough food to eat and certainly no one to care about clean clothes.

She and her sister were left for days to fend for themselves. The least of their worries was to figure out how to use a washing machine. During the worst of times, she and her sister would go to a neighbor's house for food. The Arnolds were an older couple who fed the girls, let them soak in warm bubble baths, and washed their clothes. There was always a Bible on the kitchen table, and Mrs. Arnold would sit at her piano and teach the girls to sing "Jesus Loves Me."

This couple not only told the girls about Jesus, they loved the girls and showed them genuine Christian compassion. Lisa says her first hunger to know God was as a result of the tender love and care the Arnolds expressed. The girls never felt rejected in that safe home.

However, as Lisa grew up, she felt more and more worthless. She told herself that she must be repulsively flawed if even her own parents did not love her. She was deeply ashamed of her home and her life and constantly felt an empty ache inside of longing to be loved, valued, and accepted. She tried desperately to fill the void through a sexual relationship with a teenage boy and at age fifteen discovered that she was pregnant. Her stepmother pressured her to have an abortion. At the time, Lisa thought she had no choice in the matter, so she showed up for her appointment. The family kept the abortion silent, but the pain in Lisa's heart screamed at her each day for years.

Working hard and performing well in school became a way for Lisa to feel better about herself. It also distracted her from the loss and pain the abortion caused. Teachers noticed her efforts and rewarded her with new responsibilities. In this way, for the first time in her life, Lisa felt encouraged. Her diligence at school earned her high praise and many teachers voiced high expectations for her future. But the future crashed to a screeching halt when at age seventeen she again saw the positive sign on the pregnancy test.

This time, Lisa vowed to keep the baby, but being pregnant as a high school senior carried a visible shame. She was the "responsible" student that no one ever expected to make a mistake, and it hurt knowing that she had disappointed all her teachers. Yet she never let anyone know she was hurting. She covered her pain with a smile because as a people pleaser, she feared even more rejection if people saw her pain.

Just after her daughter's first birthday, Lisa chose to marry the child's father. Two years later, she accepted Christ as her Savior and started allowing God to begin the process of healing her from her shame. She worked through a Bible study at a local pregnancy crisis center in order to deal with the guilt of her abortion. Now, ten years later, she and her husband have two precious daughters and are active in their local church.

This is not a Cinderella story, though. In the real world, there are no "happily-ever-afters." Getting better requires a lot of hard work and a continual acceptance of God's grace. For instance, Lisa initially joined a Bible study for post-abortion syndrome (PAS) to help her forgive herself and deal with the grief and guilt of her abortion. Later, she had recovered enough to serve on the staff of a crisis pregnancy center where God now uses her to guide other young women to choose life.

"Even in the darkest pit of my life, Jesus loved me," Lisa often shares. "In spite of my self and my sin, He never stopped calling me. He never stopped looking for me and pursuing me. To deny my past would be to deny Him because He has—remarkably—used it all to His glory. Each day, God fills me with hope that He will use me. Satan may have had some early victories, but Christ has won the battle! I continue seeking to understand and grow into what God wants for my life."

[handwritten margin notes: "she makes it sound too neat & simple & too easy," "not enough detail," "process description"]

Healthy Shame?

The very thought of a positive, healthy side to shame initially sent chills up and down my spine and caused severe nausea! Since shame has such a negative connotation in the area of recovery, it took a while for me to understand healthy shame and the positive purpose it serves. Although the focus of this book is not on the positive aspect of shame, you need to be aware of it.

"Biblical shame is an appropriate, healthy response when we acknowledge that we are different and less than God made us and that we are separated from Him by our sin," writes Dr. Sandra Wilson in *Released from Shame*. "Although we bear the image of God, sin radically altered our fundamental natures. Sin separates us from ourselves as originally created. Sin separates us from our original Creator."

With this perspective, consider how "healthy" shame:

this is humility, not shame.

🎀 Reminds us that we are not God.

🎀 Reminds us that to be human is to make mistakes.

🎀 Separates our behavior (what we do) from our identity (who we are).

🎀 Helps protect us from repeating painful behavior by setting boundaries with others.

🎀 Points out our need for a Savior to restore our separated relationship with God.

True Versus False Guilt

We may also experience a healthy, truthful form of spiritual shame or guilt when we feel convicted of doing something wrong. The Holy Spirit often speaks by tugging at our hearts with feelings of guilt. Jesus taught about this conviction in John 16:8: "When he (the Holy Spirit) comes, he will convict the world of guilt in regard to sin and righteousness and judgment." The Holy Spirit desires to convict us of sinful thoughts and actions so that we will pursue being changed and restored into close relationship to God through confession and repentance. He works to change the attitude of our hearts and to woo us back home.

However, many of us who have struggled with shame-based thinking and a critical conscience are easy prey for "false guilt." False guilt happens when we feel guilty for things that are not sin. We fall right back into shaming ourselves when we feel guilty for morally neutral human failures like locking keys in a car, burning the dinner casserole, or forgetting to mail a birthday card on time. People living with false guilt may use the internal nickname "stupid" on a daily basis! We say things in our self-talk that we would never dare to say out loud or to anyone else. The bottom line? False guilt is based on lies, and it does nothing but cause emotional damage.

If you showed up in my office for a counseling session, it wouldn't take long for you to figure out that my favorite verse to use in a therapy is John 8:32. In fact, all of my former clients have heard it so many times they can recite it: "You will know the truth, and the truth will set you free."

God desires to bring us truth and freedom in the inner parts of our being and thinking in order to produce healing changes. He longs to help us clean out the lies we believe, pull up the hidden roots of shame and replace them with the gentle truth and assurance of His unconditional love for us. That may seem like a foreign language here in the first chapter, but if you read to the end, I know the truth can set you free.

I've gratefully been led to that freedom in my own life, and I've seen freedom in the lives of many others. It will not happen overnight, but nothing worth keeping usually does. Instead, it will take dedication on your part and a willingness to submit to God's gentle guidance. Here are some steps that will make your journey more successful.

A Personal Invitation

In my counseling practice, I have never met a woman yet who would answer "no" to these questions: "Would you like to feel whole again? Do you long to be restored into right relationship with God? Are you longing to release your secrets in the safety of acceptance? Are you ready to trade darkness for light?" To begin a journey out of shame and into God's glory, it helps to consider these pointers from the get-go:

- ☞ Start with a commitment to read the entire book. (Getting started is easy, but sticking with it when things get uncomfortable takes commitment.)
- ☞ Make a plan for scheduled times during each week when you will have uninterrupted time to read.
- ☞ Keep a journal of your feelings as you read, and use the quiet time to search your heart for areas that need change.
- ☞ Give yourself gentle permission to put the book down for a while if a certain chapter feels overwhelming.

Through my own recovery journey and the experience of counseling many shame-filled women, I have become convinced that most of the shaming sin we get into is based on our own emotional neediness. We each desperately long to feel valuable, important, cared for, listened to, esteemed, loved, and completely accepted for who we are. We seek both to accomplish something worthwhile with our lives and to win the approval of others.

When these needs are not met, we shift into the false self and go out seeking to fill the hurting places in our hearts with relationships, activities, food, money, power, control, sex, alcohol, drugs, exercise, shopping—you name it, we've tried it. This "emotional neediness" was born out of the original sin and broken relationship with God the Father. Until we clearly understand who God truly is, how passionately He loves us, and how deeply He desires to restore us into right relationship with Him, we will continue to search for fulfillment in unsafe places.

But in this brokeness, we will never find wholeness. Restoration can only come through understanding and accepting the healing unconditional love and grace of God. We can also find remarkable hope and encouragement for our future in knowing that in Genesis 3:8-9, even after Adam and Eve had sinned, God still chose to visit the Garden that evening to search for them. God understood that Adam and Eve were the victims of their choice to disobey, and that they were now in bondage to shame, sin, secrets, darkness, and death.

Adam and Eve had changed. God had not changed at all. So with the cry of a brokenhearted Father, God called out, "Adam, where are you? Where are you?" God did not abandon His children in their time of crisis then and He has not abandoned you now.

With that same gentle understanding, God knows every minute detail of what you have done and why you are ashamed. Yet, He still lovingly pursues you at this very moment, calling out your name and asking, "My precious child, where are you?" Won't you step out of hiding and take His hand?

two

THE PARENT TRAP:
A GENERATIONAL INHERITANCE

I waited patiently for the LORD;
  he turned to me and heard my cry.
He lifted me out of the slimy pit,
  out of the mud and mire;
He set my feet on a rock
  and gave me a firm place to stand.
He put a new song in my mouth,
  a hymn of praise to our God.
                    PSALM 40:1-3

t age fifteen, I took my first job—a work crew staff position at a youth camp. I now know that "work crew" really
means slave labor in sweatshop conditions. For instance, the
camp forced my coworkers and me to work and sleep through
the 100-degree heat and humidity of a Mississippi summer with
no air conditioning. Furthermore, the director vetoed paper
plates and plastic forks, so we washed piles of dishes by hand
at every meal. We also cleaned the snack shop, changed the
sheets for the guest speakers, and swept mountains of dead
horse flies (thank goodness some of them actually died before
having a chance to bite me) from the perpetually filthy dining

hall floors. The camp assigned us many other yucky jobs that no one else wanted to do.

As a teenager, I actually thought it was a lot of fun, and I couldn't believe they were willing to pay me thirty-five dollars a week for the pleasure of working there! However, the most fun happened when we teens would sort of stretch, uh, well . . . you know, sort of break curfew to roam around after everyone else had gone to bed.

One of our favorite endeavors was to see how many of us could cram ourselves like human sardines into the cab and bed of an old Datsun pickup truck. Once in it, we drove around the lake at night in search of deer. When our headlights hit them, they were immediately blinded and paralyzed with fear. We got a kick out of harmlessly "catching" them this way. Many deer die in night traffic because when they see the oncoming balls of light, they freeze, not knowing what to do or where to run.

Years later, as I looked at the client seated in my counseling office, it dawned on me that Wanda had the classic deer-in-the-headlights look of panic. She first arrived at the Minirth-Meier Clinic in Dallas, Texas, on a chilly November day dressed in a professionally tailored navy suit. As part of her austere image, she wore her thin brown hair pulled back from her face in a severe twist. This hairstyle fully revealed both her lovely peaches-and-cream complexion as well as the dark circles under her eyes. Though pretty, Wanda looked weary with the burdens of life, and I noticed that she never arrived without her briefcase in tow. After several months of counseling, she decided to talk about her father.

"I'm not really comfortable talking about my father," she began. "My earliest memories of him are that we never knew where he was, or when he would come home. My mother seemed constantly on edge, anxious, and fearful, and I can remember clinging to her skirt to hide, when he finally came home."

"What were you afraid of?" I gently asked.

"I, uh, I don't really know," she stammered. "He was not an

angry man, but he was always drunk. Sometimes he was in jail for public drunkenness. He was strangely distant; he never played with me, talked to me, nor came to any of my school functions. He seemed to spend every penny on his precious alcohol! It didn't take long to understand that he loved alcohol more than he loved anything else. I remember my mother crying because there was no food in the house," she said and then paused.

"Sometimes all we had for days was potatoes or rice. When everything ran out, she would send us to the local pastor to beg for food. It was humiliating to repeatedly ask for help. My father would rather spend money on another drink than feed us." By now, Wanda's fair face flushed red with anger. She continued speaking through clenched teeth.

"I vowed that I would never take a drink of alcohol, and I never have! I'm the only person in my family to ever receive a college degree, which by the way, I completed in three years. Since then, I have worked hard to climb the corporate ladder and I've earned many promotions. I make certain my family has all its needs met. My children are well fed and they will never lose me to alcohol, no matter what!"

The aforementioned deer-in-the-headlights look came into her eyes when she emphatically made this declaration. A moment later, I watched a light bulb flicker on in her mind. For the first time, Wanda actually heard what she had said, and she connected with it. Powerful revelations are rarely foreign to a struggling person. It's as if the insight has always been there, but the client has pushed it far away because facing the root problem can be painful. Not surprisingly, Wanda put her head down and began to sob.

"I feel so ashamed of myself," she whispered between gasps for air. For a few seconds I said nothing, and instead, waited to see if she had more to say.

"Tell me about the tears," I finally entreated, breaking the silence. With her head in her hands, Wanda shook her head as in disbelief and responded.

"It's me. It's me! I've been so proud of never taking a drink, but I suddenly realized that I am just like my father! I've never been at home either. I feel so angry about his alcoholism, but I think I must be a workaholic. I swore I would be different from him, but I'm not. My whole life is wrapped up in my job. I only feel good if I'm performing well at work," she cried.

could i possibly be a wanna be workaholic?

"My children and husband must feel left out. I really haven't met all their needs, just the physical ones. No wonder they are always bugging me to slow down or take a vacation with them. In a way, I've been just like my father, and I couldn't stand him! How could I have ever let this happen?" she concluded.

Some family legacies leave us feeling ashamed of our parents' behavior, ashamed of what people in the church or community think of us, ashamed of our last name, ashamed of whom we belong to, and ashamed of who we perceive ourselves to be. Like Wanda, people in this boat want to somehow vanish and hide when someone says with disdain, "Oh, you're Joe's daughter." They know full well that the smirk means, "You belong to that no good alcoholic who can't stay out of jail."

Tangible Inheritances

Some days stand out more than others. June 28, 1998, is one of those days for me. While visiting my parents in Birmingham, Alabama, I took my two-year-old son, Christian, and my five-year-old daughter, Elisabeth, to see Marion Spell, my ninety-six-year-old grandmother who resided in Georgetown, Mississippi. Her health had been in decline, and we had not been able to visit her in more than a year.

In my mind's eye, I still imagined her to be the vibrant sixty-year-old of my youth, so it was shocking to find her looking smaller and more frail than ever. Nevertheless, she and I enjoyed watching my children play, as we laughed about similar antics I exhibited when I was their age. So, it surprised me when, in the midst of the carefree afternoon, my grandmother slipped into a serious mood, reached into her pocket and brought forth her diamond cluster ring.

"Your grandfather gave me this in 1972 on our fiftieth wedding anniversary," she said with great tenderness in her voice as she remembered the past. "Now I want you to have it."

"Please, Grandmother," I protested, tears welling up in my eyes. "I don't want it yet. You keep it for now." But she refused.

"I can't wear it anymore," she explained, "and I want to know that you have it."

That afternoon proved very special for both of us. Who knew that this heirloom exchange would represent our last meaningful interaction before she went home to be with the Lord later that year in October? Owning her ring gives me a special comfort as I wear it each day and think of her. When my daughter is grown, I plan to give the ring to her as a tangible inheritance of our family's love and history.

Intangible Inheritances

Tangible inheritances come in many forms such as heirlooms, stock, land, homes, and money. While not everyone enjoys the privilege of receiving a material inheritance, everyone receives an intangible inheritance. For instance, some are blessed with healthy, positive family interaction. Others may feel cursed by an intergenerational chain of dysfunction involving codependency, broken relationships, incest, abuse, neglect, or substance abuse.

Dysfunctional families often keep secrets that go back for many generations. These secrets are kept due to the shame that surrounds them. Typically, secrets revolve around divorce, abortion, incest, children born of incest, children otherwise born out of wedlock, suicides, homicides, addictions, and even bankruptcy.

Secrets become very powerful because other family members cannot change what they do not know. Consequently, a dysfunctional family is as sick as its secrets. A family will only be able to drain power from those secrets by acknowledging and exposing them.

The Bible clearly addresses the concept of generational sin. For instance, in the middle of the Ten Commandments (Exodus 20:5-6), God says: "For I, the LORD your God, am a jealous God, punishing the children for the sin of the fathers to the third and fourth generation of those who hate me, but showing love to a thousand generations of those who love me and keep my commandments."

Later, in Exodus 34:6-7, God repeats: "The LORD, the compassionate and gracious God, slow to anger, abounding in love and faithfulness, maintaining love to thousands, and forgiving wickedness, rebellion, and sin. Yet he does not leave the guilty unpunished; he punishes the children and their children for the sin of the fathers to the third and fourth generation."

No wonder a psychologist I know once said, "Ninety-five percent of families are dysfunctional, and we can't find the other five percent." That line can produce a good laugh, but the term "dysfunctional families" has been tossed around so much that its meaning is now fuzzy. In reality we are *all* dysfunctional due to our various imperfections. The question is, to what degree?

Nationally known Christian psychiatrist and author Dr. Frank Minirth writes, "All families are somewhat codependent or dysfunctional. That's natural, since none of us is perfect. All of our parents have made some mistakes and passed some of their pain on to us, and we'll pass some of that pain on to our own children."[1]

I define dysfunction as anyone who is "human, prone to make mistakes, needy, self-centered, hurting, sinful, and damaged by the sins of others." Because we are all frail human beings, we tend to unwittingly pass our character flaws and sinful tendencies on to our children.

For instance, many adults of dysfunctional families assert that they will never repeat the annoying or hurtful things their parents said to them. Then, during a weak moment of extreme frustration with a child, they open their mouth and their mother or father's words fall out! I knew I was in trouble when I asked my three-year-old, "Young lady, do you want me to spank you right now?" Yikes! I had just rewound one of those dreaded old tapes from my parents and played it back to my child.

Nonetheless, it's tempting to fool yourself into believing that you can create a better life for your children—without addressing and resolving your own dysfunctional issues. The truth is that if you die with only five dollars to your name, your child will only inherit five dollars. You cannot pass on something to your children that you do not have.

INDIVIDUAL FORMATION

Someone once noted that children are "wet cement." The components of the cement are already determined, but the shape into which the cement forms is yet to be decided. In the same way, at birth the temperament of the child has already been genetically determined. The patterns that will be stamped into the "wet cement" of their lives depend on the influence of parents, relatives, and peers, as well as a host of circumstances and choices.

Keep in mind that whatever your family situation—positive or negative—it will seem normal to you because that unique stamp has been molded onto your wet cement. Furthermore, without exposure to more healthy examples, even highly dysfunctional families regard certain behaviors as typical. For instance, if your father is physically abusive, you may incorrectly assume that all fathers abuse their children.

When family circumstances prove painful, many tend to blame themselves and accept the darkness of shame. They feel responsible for the situation and believe that they must be flawed. Otherwise, this would not be happening in their home.

Furthermore, individuals who grow up in shaming, dysfunctional homes quickly learn unspoken rules. Do you recognize any of these, the most common unspoken rules in dysfunctional families?

🍃 **Feel nothing.** Instead, hide your emotions—especially sadness and anger—and avoid expressing any feelings, needs, or wants.

🍃 **Stay in control.** "Never let them see you cry," becomes the motto. Work hard to hide anything in your life perceived as a weakness.

🍃 **Work to be perfect.** If you do everything right, then you may be able to solve the problems in your family or at least receive the love you so desperately desire.

🍃 **Deny, deny, deny.** Lie to yourself and those around you by pretending that there are no problems. Another form of denial involves trying to be someone you are not in order to gain acceptance.

🍃 **Do not trust.** Avoid trusting yourself or others, because any gut feeling you have "must be wrong."

🍃 **Maintain the secrecy.** Share the secrets of your family with no one. After all, even if you dared, who would listen or believe you?

🍃 **Feel ashamed.** You believe you are actually powerful enough to cause the bad things that happen, so everything negative must be your fault. Therefore, you deserve abuse and/or neglect.

CONFUSING INHERITANCES

Growing up, I always had a crush on Elvis Presley. I even had a large poster of him on my closet door and a collection of thirty-six of his albums. During my own struggles with depression, I would often feel better after listening to his upbeat songs. So it was shocking after his death to learn that he had so many problems with insecurity, loneliness, and drug addiction.

Today, I wish I could somehow rewind the clock and sit down in a counseling room with Elvis and his parents. What were the effects of poverty on the family? How did his mother deal with the death of Elvis's twin brother? How did the family handle the months when his father was in jail?

What was it like to suddenly move from this desolate lifestyle into wealth and a spotlight where millions of people idolized him with expectations so intense that he became a recluse? How does it affect the human psyche to become the object of worship and idolatry? No one will ever get the chance to counsel Elvis and his family. But you don't need to read too many of his biographies to see that something—maybe many things—went terribly wrong in his family to produce such severe heartache in the midst of such fabulous success.

GENERATIONAL SIN CLOSE UP

Recently, I boarded a 5:45 A.M. flight on my way to a speaking engagement at a women's retreat. My goal was to catch up on my sleep during the commute, but God had another idea. As I squished into my window seat, an elderly gentleman went out of his way to hold my coat and coffee. Our conversation started quickly as I sat down beside "John." I noticed that John wasn't prepared like the typical traveler. He had no book or magazine in tow.

Turns out he had left rather hastily. He told me that he was going to the bedside of his older brother who was in a coma. John had not seen him in sixteen years. Besides the stress related to that crisis, John felt exhausted from visiting his granddaughter in the hospital hours before catching this early flight. She had just delivered her third child out of wedlock and, due to complications, the child's life was in danger.

He gravely explained that the baby's parents did not want anything to do with her. However, he wanted to show support and see the infant before he left for what was certain to be his brother's funeral. At that point, I asked if he had support from his wife, and he chuckled bitterly.

"My wife," he paused, "she died six years ago."

"I am so sorry," I responded.

"Oh don't be sorry," John replied. "We divorced twenty years ago. We were both alcoholics, and I finally kicked her out. I don't do much drinking any more, and I'm not lonely for the ladies. But I do wish my children would talk to me."

Finally, I asked John about his parents. Again came that bitter laugh. He explained that he had never met his father, and that his mother was preparing to marry for the thirteenth time before she died last year at the age of ninety-three.

I felt such sorrow for John due to the damage of generational sin he had just described. Just trying to sort out who did what felt overwhelming. But God was gracious, and John's heart was open when I shared about the redeeming love of Christ. I will probably never know what happened to him, but I can continue to pray for him. Your life may not be as painful as his, but we are all products of the past.

A Biblical Example

The family of Abraham and Sarah and the following generations described in Genesis, chapters twelve through fifty, would give any therapist plenty of generational sin-related case studies. For instance, as Abraham and his wife, Sarah, entered Egypt, he called her his sister to increase his chances of survival. After all, if he admitted that he was her husband, the Egyptians might kill him in order to solicit her unhindered. The plan worked for a while until the pharaoh uncovered the secret and kicked them out of town.

Another time, Abraham and Sarah tried desperately to have a child with no success. So Sarah suggested that Abraham should have a child with her servant Hagar. According to the custom then, Hagar's offspring would be Sarah's property. (I personally like this idea of surrogate mothers—it sounds much less painful than the real thing!) Anyway, Hagar delivered a child named Ishmael, and he was considered Sarah's son.

Life went on peacefully until Sarah, at age eighty-nine, conceived and gave birth to Isaac. Conflict then began to brew as Sarah became jealous and resentful of the attention Abraham continued to give Hagar and Ishmael. So she pushed Abraham to choose a favorite son, and of course he chose Isaac.

With this couple, dysfunctional family patterns began emerging and ultimately were replicated in subsequent generations. What might those patterns be? First, when in trouble, try to lie your way out of it. Also, show unfair favoritism, no matter how hurtful that may be to other family members. After all, Isaac grew up and married Rebekah. They eventually settled in a foreign city where—just like dear old Dad—Isaac lied by telling everyone that Rebekah was his sister because he feared someone would kill him in order to have her.

Shortly thereafter, Rebekah gives birth to twin boys—Esau and Jacob. These fellows come out of the womb and immediately exhibit totally opposite temperaments. Esau becomes a big, rugged "man's man" who likes to hunt. Isaac is proud of him and begins to show the favoritism that runs in his family. Jacob, on the other hand, is more the quiet indoors type. He enjoys talking with his mother and cooking with her. Soon, she shows favoritism to him.

When Isaac was old and blind, he was ready to give the blessing of inheritance to Esau, but Rebekah and Jacob plotted a scheme of deceit. They lied to Isaac and stole the blessing for Jacob. (Is this starting to sound like television's *Peyton Place?*) Jacob had to run for his life to escape the wrath of Esau. Jacob eventually married two sisters and showed favoritism to Rachel, then later, to Joseph, Rachel's firstborn son.

This dark legacy of deceit and favoritism continues as Jacob gave Joseph the coat of many colors. He might as well have given him a banner stating: "I AM DAD'S FAVORITE SON." I only have three children, but I can't imagine the uproar that would happen if I gave only one child a spectacular coat and left out the other two. I would never hear the end of it.

It was no surprise, then, that the other brothers felt a surge of jealousy toward their baby brother. In fact, they became so outraged by the favoritism shown toward Joseph, that they plotted to murder him and eventually settled on selling him into slavery with the Egyptians. The brothers returned home after doing this and lied to Jacob. They told him that a wild animal killed Joseph.

Each generation repeated problems that had started in previous generations. A chain of codependency formed and each family added new links to the chain. The great hope in this story occurs in the fourth generation when Joseph trusts God to guide him. In this way, he broke the chain and lived a life of freedom in God's truth. In every situation Joseph faced, he turned to God for wisdom instead of following after his own needs and emotions.

Joseph later comes face to face with his brothers. Instead of being filled with bitterness and wishing to avenge himself for their past hatred of him, he offers them forgiveness. For this reason, he makes a great Old Testament example of Romans 8:28—that God can eventually use all the things we go through in life to produce something positive. Joseph declares, "You intended to harm me, but God intended it for good to accomplish what is now being done" (Genesis 50:20).

Family Roles

Just as actors get cast in specific roles, family members can also play roles in the family system. In dysfunctional families, these roles involve habitually demonstrating behaviors, feelings, actions, and responses that shame one's "true self" and squelch the freedom to authentically respond to circumstances. Instead, this family member feels obligated to make the choices that others expect or demand. Family members caught in this trap often develop a "false self" and learn to hide in these expected roles. Ultimately, these roles allow the family member to fit into the family system and avoid rejection, particularly when that rejection comes from a caregiver.

Unfortunately, playing an expected role robs you of your unique giftedness as an individual created by God. Also, if you practice these roles long enough, you won't be able to discern the difference between your false self and your genuine self. Instead, you'll be indefinitely typecast as the scapegoat, clown, black sheep, baby, rescuer, confessor, emotional spouse, and so on.

Can you identify the roles you played in your family while growing up, and how that acting affects you today? Until you understand those roles, you will stay stuck in them and may very likely repeat the same unhealthy dynamics in your current family. Dr. Robert Hemfelt describes repeating the past as a homing instinct in humans. "Rather than seek out physically the place of our childhood, we seek to reconstruct it in our present life. We all possess a primal need to recreate the familiar, the original family situation, *even if the familiar, the situation, is destructive and painful.*"[2]

So, until you understand the roles of each family member and how they interacted, you will continue to dramatically or subtly repeat your family's generational patterns. You are not responsible for the negative things that happened to you during childhood. Those things were out of your control. But you are responsible as an adult to make choices about how you will live your life. You can choose to remain a victim. You can continue feeding the anger inside. You can remain trapped in addiction. Or, you can choose to change and pursue being emotionally and spiritually mature and healthy.

Who Is God?

All children are egocentric. That means they think the world revolves around them, and that they are powerful enough to control the things that happen around them. If Dad happens to come home from work in a bad mood and yells at the child, the child does not have the ability to think, "Dad has had a bad day at work."

Let's face it, most of us as adults have a hard time separating ourselves from the moods and actions of others. So, it should be no surprise that children are not able to detach from the actions of their parents. Rather, the child internalizes these actions, and wonders what she did wrong to cause the father to be so angry. This disturbing internal feeling becomes fertile soil for the seeds of shame to begin growing.

Children begin to assume that there is something horribly wrong with them. They don't understand that there may be other reasons a parent is yelling at them. Because of this, the child may start to believe that good behavior can win love. Trying harder for perfection then becomes an unconscious drive at the core of this child, and it reinforces the idea that she is flawed, damaged, and unworthy of love and acceptance.

During childhood, we develop ideas about who we are. We also begin to develop ideas about who God is. When my children say their prayers at night, I often wonder if their little minds are actually thinking, "Dear heavenly version of my earthly Father." To children, parents represent God—physical giants who provide food, clothing, shelter, attention, and love. Without the support of parents, children are helpless. No wonder, then, that parents hold absolute power in the eyes of their children. However skewed, kids commonly place the head of a parent on the shoulders of God.

If you grow up with a verbally abusive parent, chances are that you view God as critical. A perfectionistic parent represents a perpetually unsatisfied God. So, if your parent is a perfectionist, you may feel unable to please God—despite your best efforts. If you were physically or emotionally abandoned, you may doubt God's desire for a relationship. Distant or workaholic parents often produce a child who thinks God is too busy and detached to care about her individual needs.

Children who have legalistic or rule-bound parents may desperately try to achieve in order to earn the love of God. Within this paradigm, they feel like they always fail and might as well stop trying. For them, faith—like just about everything else—is an "all or nothing" proposition. Since no one can be "all" before God, the child gives up the struggle and believes the shameful lie that she is "nothing." A sexually abused child may wonder where God was during the violations and why life continues to be so painful. If God cares, why didn't He rescue her from the horror of her torture?

In these ways, dysfunctional families give children distorted images—lies—about God. Replacing those lies with the truth about God often involves a long and painful process, but it's well worth the struggle!

Hope for Change

I mentioned in chapter 1 that my favorite verse is John 8:32: "You will know the truth, and the truth will set you free." In my own recovery, I have learned that practicing the truth about how God views me has worked to heal hurts and has reformed my dysfunctional belief system into something healthier. Viewed simply, this verse means that truth equals freedom and lies equal bondage.

Who wouldn't desire to live and walk in the freedom of God's truth and unconditional love? But, many get tangled up in the lies of Satan, and they remain in painful bondage. Such generational inheritances can involve emotional, physical, and spiritual bondage.

Jesus said, "I am the way, the truth and the life. No one comes to the Father except through me" (John 14:6). Wow! The Truth has been revealed to us in the person of Jesus Christ! What a comfort to learn that the more intimate we become in our relationship with Jesus, the more we will know about the truth. Understanding your intangible family inheritance, coupled with Christ's liberating power, you can say today, "The buck stops with me."

three

THE MURDER OF A SOUL: DAMAGES OF ABUSE

$\mathcal{R}$eading comics in the Sunday paper is a great way to get a chuckle! One of my favorite strips has always been *Peanuts*, by Charles Schultz. Maybe one of the reasons I like it so much is because I played Lucy Van Pelt in the musical, *You're a Good Man Charlie Brown*, when I was a junior in high school. As this character, others applauded me for being sarcastic, rude, mean, and generally in a foul mood! That never has happened before or since, and reminiscing about it still makes me grin. I certainly wish my family would clap for me when I get into those moods now, but somehow that is never their response.

Pigpen is another memorable character in the *Peanuts* gang. He is the little fellow who is constantly shrouded in a cloud of dirt and dust. Wherever Pigpen goes, the cloud is sure to follow. It seems like he has been dirty for so long, that he's permanently stained; no amount of scrubbing with Lava soap could clean that kid! A bath for him would merely create a huge mud puddle.

Shame feels a lot like Pigpen looks. Often, the cloud that always hovers near includes fear, anxiety, loneliness, guilt over past sin, depression, sadness, a bitter spirit toward those who damaged you, the shame of addiction, a painful divorce, and rejection.

Pigpen seems isolated from others at times. No one wants to eat the simple dirty lemon drops, which are the only thing he has to offer. If I were Pigpen, I would feel rejected and probably think, "Why should I bother to change anyway? If they don't like me now, they won't like me clean either. Besides, I feel pretty comfortable here in my own dirt. Others may not come around, but that just spares me from one more rejection."

Understanding Abuse

Children experience various types of abuse. Some forms are obvious. Other forms are subtle. But all abuse is a form of abandonment, because when a child is abused, no one is there to meet the child's needs. Worse yet, adults often tell the children they abuse that this treatment is for their own good. However, in truth, abuse is *always* about the perpetrator and *never* about the child. In fact, abusive behavior points directly back to the adult's own unresolved issues. Unfortunately, though the child is not responsible for the abuse, it heaps shame onto the child—sometimes for a lifetime.

In their naturally egocentric thinking, children make themselves responsible for the abuse. Believing that their caregiver/god could be emotionally sick or even crazy would make the child's world completely unstable. For instance, the child fears she cannot survive with a crazy parent. Because she is completely dependent on the power of the caregiver, the child internalizes the abuse and shame and thinks: "*I* must be crazy. Something must be very wrong with me or my caregiver wouldn't have to treat me this way. This is entirely my fault. I must try harder to be good."

Once the child internalizes this lie, the seed of shame and destruction spreads its roots rapidly and deeply into every crevice of the child's emotions, needs, and wants. This cancer of shame will continue to grow and stain every area it touches until as an adult, with the help of God and His truth, the person is able to form a defense plan and yell: "Halt! I've had enough!"

Of course, even the most wonderful parent will blow it occasionally due to frustration or ignorance. That is a given for all human beings. What separates a rare mistake from damaging abuse is the degree and frequency. A temporary outburst may sting, but a loving safe relationship will quickly flow again between parent and child. However, continual abuse creates permanent scars and causes a child to shut down emotionally. And parents aren't the only perpetrators. Abuse can occur at the hands of foster parents, a relative, mentor, coach, teacher, spiritual leader, an older sibling and his or her peers, or a babysitter.

Abuse falls into two categories: active or passive. The effects of active abuse are more obvious than those of passive abuse. In fact, it often takes lots of digging to recognize passive abuse. Identifying a broken arm will always be easier than identifying a rejected soul.

Nevertheless, abuse need not cause permanent damage. The wounds are certainly painful, and many leave scars. But the damage is not irreversible. Remember the story of Jacob's son

Joseph? Joseph had good reasons to give up hope due to abandonment and abuse:

☞ His mother died during his childhood.
☞ His father overprotected him as the favorite son.
☞ His brothers expressed open hatred for him.
☞ He was sold into slavery.
☞ He suffered for years as a slave, and was even put in prison.

Yet, when he finally stepped into a powerful position of authority, when he could have taken revenge on his brothers for their abusiveness, he forgave them and reunited with his father.

To recover, abused people must deal with the past through a similar healing process that involves forgiveness. Webster's dictionary defines "process" as "a continuing development involving many changes; a particular method of doing something, with all the steps involved." Not surprisingly, healing takes time. But you cannot change what you have not recognized. So the first step in the recovery process involves identifying the various areas of abuse in its two major categories—active and passive.

Abuse Types

I. ACTIVE ABUSE

Physical Abuse

Highly dysfunctional families often accept violence and rage as a normal dynamic. Physical abuse includes hitting, slapping, pinching, kicking, pushing, pulling, shaking, choking, and being tortured with non-stop tickling. It also includes ritualistic abuse such as repetitive acts planned to produce pain and suffering to a child.

Furthermore, witnessing an act of violence does the same damage to a child as experiencing the violence firsthand. If a child watches her mother or sibling being beaten or raped, the damage is equal to the child being beaten or raped.

Most abusers are impulsive and unpredictable. Therefore, victims learn to be helpless in defending themselves. They can no longer plan an escape or think to protect themselves. Instead, they learn to passively accept the abuse.

Sometimes, a rejected child will actually irritate the parent in order to get attention. Why? Neglected children would rather be hit than not touched at all. For some, the only physical touch they ever receive is a spanking. If the child cannot get this need for touch met in one way or another, the child may eventually lose awareness of those needs. This is the client who enters my office as an adult, not knowing what she needs or how she feels.

Sexual Abuse

Sexuality is a natural, God-given desire. However, when someone violates another person's sexual boundaries, it wounds that person to the core. For this reason, I believe that sexual abuse is the most damaging and shaming of all abuses. Yet, it is so horribly common in our culture. I have devoted chapter 6 to addressing this issue in more detail.

Sexual abuse includes any touching, hugging, or kissing that is in any way sexual. It involves fondling, oral or anal sex, masturbating the victim or forcing the victim to masturbate the abuser, and intercourse.

Active Verbal Abuse

Physical abuse and sexual abuse are both illegal. Although there are no laws against verbal violence, it remains an active and destructive form of abuse. Raging shrieks leave bruises that will never be seen, but are painfully felt. Obvious examples include comments like, "You never do anything right! You will never amount to anything. I wish you had never been born! My life was good before you came along! Get out of this room, you stupid idiot! You ruin everything! You make me sick!"

Several years ago, I witnessed a more subtle form of verbal abuse. I was visiting in the home of a family with a thirteen-year-old son. The mother told me that they were having problems getting their son to communicate with them. She reported that he seemed silent and withdrawn, and that when he did talk, he was sarcastic and angry. She wondered what was going on with him.

Minutes later, the boy called from another room to ask for help with the model ship he was building. As we entered the room, he was trying to detail the ship with long strips of decal stickers. His mother immediately took the model out of his hands and said, "You never do this straight. Why do you even bother trying to build a model if you can't get the stripes on correctly?" I watched the boy's spirit shrivel up. No wonder he found it difficult to communicate with his mother! I couldn't blame him. Who wants to spend time talking with a critic?

II. PASSIVE ABUSE

Abandonment

Abandonment means to be left alone. This happens when a parent is physically absent, but it can also happen when they are physically present. Abandonment occurs when the child's basic physical and emotional needs go unmet. Physical needs include food and water, shelter, and clothing, as well as care during illness or injury. In addition, every child needs love, acceptance, and affirmation. Sadly, many forms of passive abuse are never identified as such. Alcoholism, drug abuse, sexual addiction, gambling, and workaholism explain why some parents fail to meet their child's needs.

In this case, the sin may very likely be generational. For instance, emotionally frozen parents probably grew up in a stoic home where emotional expression was discouraged. Therefore, they follow that pattern with their children. When a physically present parent abandons a child emotionally, the child feels unstable and desperate for affirmation.

In this way, an emotionally unavailable father unwittingly pushes a little girl to go to great lengths to get his attention. She may strive to be a tomboy or compete in his favorite sports and hobbies. She may develop into a perfectionistic people pleaser forever bent on trying harder.

> There are other forms of passive abuse. Unintentional or unavoidable though they may be, the effects remain the same. Abandonment is abusive, and make no mistake, divorce, however amicable, is abandonment. The long absences of a father in the military service is abandonment. So is premature death of a parent. The abandonment may be necessary, as with the military man. It may be unintentional or unavoidable, as for example, an accidental death. But to the child's subconscious, it is abandonment nonetheless.[1]

When a parent consistently tells a child to go away, that child has been abandoned even though the parent is physically present. This type of parent probably believes that "Children should be seen and not heard." So, the parent interacts with the child with these kinds of statements: "Go in the other room and find something to do. I'm too tired to play right now. Hey, can't you see I'm watching the ballgame? Get out of here. No you can't help me. You will only make another mess."

Remember, because your own home feels "normal" to you, it is often difficult to identify passive abuse. The main question to ask is, "Were my parents available for me?"

Passive Verbal Abuse

In this case, parents never angrily shout or berate their children. They just fail to verbalize affirmations, encouragement, and expressions of joy. I have counseled several women whose parents were never harsh, but they never once heard them say anything tender like, "I'm glad you are mine. You did a great job! I am so proud of you." Most importantly, these women missed hearing "I love you."

While never abusively criticized, these children feel more or less ignored. As a result, these children often feel unlovable, insignificant, and worthless.

Other Passive Abuses

Children feel secure when they know their parents have a strong bond and show loving affection toward each other. Parents who do not love each other passively abuse their children. The children recognize that the marriage is unstable and may break up at any moment. So they work hard trying to "fix" things for the parents. They try to draw attention away from the parental discord by creating new problems with acting-out behaviors.

Perfectionistic or compulsive parents also passively abuse their children by demanding that same type of behavior from them. For instance, children who watch their mother vacuum the carpet twice a day understand that modeling this type of compulsive behavior will please her, even though it's unhealthy for everyone.

Finally, chronically depressed parents create another passively abusive situation because they often cannot meet the child's needs. The child realizes this and typically assumes a caregiver role to try to meet the parent's needs.

Spiritual Abuse

Spiritual abuse happens when a person uses the Bible or the name of God in order to manipulate. As a Christian counselor, I have seen many clients who are damaged by this type of passive abuse. Feelings of anger or sexuality are the emotions most often criticized and rejected as anti-Christian.

Yet, spiritual abuse is difficult to confront because it is disguised as part of a "spiritual" upbringing. One of my clients told me that whenever she disobeyed, she was required to sit for hours and write out chapters of the Bible. Others heard manipulative comments like, "God will get you for that. If you do that again, God will not love you. When you act that way, God is so disappointed, He can't even look at you. God told me to send you to your room with no dinner. God doesn't like little girls who get angry. Sin will send you to hell."

Churches are also capable of abuse when a pastor demands complete authority over a congregation. Children learn that they are not allowed to question anything he says. They are required to offer "blind obedience." Legalism, which requires complete adherence to all church rules, sets a child up to work for the approval of a strict and unloving God.

Grace is rarely mentioned in homes and churches where people spiritually abuse. So, to the children, God naturally becomes the cosmic boogieman waiting to zap them if they make a mistake. They learn that God is always angry and lurking to catch them doing something wrong.

In this way, a distorted belief system forms, telling them that because they are so bad, God would surely not want anything to do with them. If they do something wrong, they will surely go to hell. God's love—as spiritually abused children understand it—must be earned through working to perfectly obey all the rules. Ultimately, spiritual abusers convey a deep message of shame that causes them to believe that God will never love them because they are so bad.

Is it any wonder that many of these children reject God and rebel against religion as adults? These victims can only reestablish a healthy relationship with God as they learn the truth of God's unconditional love.

Finally, spiritual abusers shame and hurt others when they teach that Christians should not seek counseling for emotional problems.

Emotional Incest

In this case, the word incest is not about sexual abuse. It is used here because emotional incest is a serious form of abuse in which the role of parent and child are reversed. The child becomes a surrogate parent or spouse for a parent. This type of passive abuse forces the child to assume the role of an adult in subtle and elusive ways. Emotional incest is very serious because it involves distortion of appropriate family roles.

The parent unconsciously thinks, "I don't really like my spouse, but that's all right since I have this wonderful child that I love more than anyone else." This really means, "I am not getting my needs met in this marriage, but my child can meet those needs." Were you always there to meet the needs of your mother, father, or both? Did your parents bond inappropriately with you? Were you allowed to have a childhood, or were you expected to be a miniature adult? If you answered "yes" to any of these questions, you may have emotional incest in your family.

This type of passive abuse can also occur when a parent pushes a child to take over household chores such as cooking, cleaning, or childcare because the parent is absent, sick, or preoccupied. The parent may also manipulate the child into becoming a friend, confidant, and emotional caretaker. When a child is told things about the other parent that are inappropriate for a child, this is emotional incest.

I remember a client whose mother regularly shared all the details of the father's extramarital affairs. This unhappy mother even asked the child for advice about how to be more sexually attractive to the father. Clearly, the mother was using the child to get her emotional needs met. The parent in this situation is a "bottomless pit" of emotional neediness, so she siphons every ounce of emotional energy and love that the child has to offer.

Of course, the child believes that this is a "normal" situation and also wants to please the parent. The tragedy is that, at a time when the child needs love and nurture poured in, the child is instead being drained. This type of behavior is an example of cross-generational bonding. Children become enmeshed with a parent when they take on the covert needs of that parent. This enmeshment blends boundaries, so the child becomes uncertain of where she begins and the parent ends. In every case, the child experiences abandonment because she needs a relationship with a parent—not a confidant or spouse.

Another form of emotional incest occurs when a parent lives vicariously through the life of the child. Maybe the mother was never able to dance so she pushes the daughter to be a ballerina, even when the child is not interested. The mother may say, "I never had a chance to do these things, so you are going to do it and enjoy it." In this way, the mother uses the child to fulfill her unresolved dreams.

Abuse Fallout

Abused and/or neglected children eventually learn to believe that their needs are unimportant. They lose any sense of personal value and may also ultimately decide that no one is dependable or trustworthy. Children with this background view their neediness as shameful. But, since these basic needs are God-given, they never just evaporate. So, the abused or neglected child typically turns to unhealthy substitutes for getting those needs met. Abuse leads that child to believe:

- 🐞 I am bad and rotten to the core. No matter how hard I try, I will always be bad.
- 🐞 Maybe if I can be perfect, my parent will love me.
- 🐞 Love always hurts, but parents only hurt you because they want you to be good.
- 🐞 Anger is sin. I must never be angry, or I will hurt someone.
- 🐞 I am so sinful that God will never love me.
- 🐞 I can't tell people who I really am, or they will reject me.
- 🐞 I must pretend to be better.

Broken Boundaries

As I mentioned earlier, abuse confuses children. They lose track of where they start and the parent ends. Parent and child become pathologically enmeshed. In this case, the child often believes that she is responsible for the feelings and actions of the parent. In her confusion, the child doesn't know how to say "no" or when to say "yes." The child grows into an adult who tries to rescue others instead of letting others take care of themselves. Furthermore, this damaged adult will manipulate others into taking care of her when she needs to be responsible. Dr. Henry Townsend wrote,

> Boundaries, in a broad sense, are lines or things that mark a limit, bound, or border. In a psychological sense, boundaries are the realization of our own persona apart from others. This sense of separateness forms the basis of personal identity. It says what we are and what we are not, what we will endure and what we will not, what we feel and what we will not feel, what we like, and what we do not like, and what we want and what we do not want. Boundaries, in short, define us. In the same way that a physical boundary defines where a property line begins and ends, a psychological and spiritual boundary defines who we are and who we are not.[2]

Abuse breaks down boundaries and makes each victim uncertain of what healthy boundaries would even look like.

False and True Self Development

Many marvel over the knowledge that no two snowflakes are ever alike. Snowflakes are an amazing creation, but human beings are phenomenal when compared to any other part of creation. God has taken the time to give us our own unique set of fingerprints. Greater still, He created us in His image! But many grow up never appreciating the wonder of their special design.

We are born into the world with what I call the "true self." The true self is not afraid of expressing emotions and needs. Creativity, spontaneity, and honesty reside in the true self during childhood. We feel safe enough to trust enough to allow ourselves to be vulnerable and intimate with others.

Think for a moment about a three-year-old child. You know when children that age think something is funny because they erupt into spontaneous, pure laughter that makes everyone else in the room laugh. They openly express anger and frustration when their plans are blocked. I recall a time when I was stuck at an airport with my children during a long delay and they started to cry from their own fatigue and frustration. At times like that, I wish I could break down and cry with them. But that would not be considered "acceptable behavior" for an adult in a public place.

I like to watch children in the grocery store. There they sit, perched in the shopping cart. As people pass by, they break out their most charming ear-to-ear grin and say, "Hi!" When is the last time you smiled at someone and said "Hi!" while grocery shopping? Most are too busy trying to get ahead in line to bother with smiling, let alone speaking. Besides, didn't I read somewhere that shopping with the fastest checkout time is a new Olympic sporting event?

Elevators are no better. My kids would have no problem striking up a conversation in any elevator with anybody, but we grownups seem to have another set of rules. Have you noticed how adults pile in without speaking? We all face the front, tilt our heads up and stare—mesmerized—at the numbers while we wait for our floor of departure. Is there an invisible sign I've missed that says, "Absolutely no talking in elevators"?

So, the set of rules we live by in adult life often involves acting through a "false self." Abused and neglected adults develop a much more extensive false self because they determine uncon-sciously that the true self is not meeting their needs or keeping them protected enough. So, the victim begins building a façade in order to survive.

For example, in some homes a child may be scolded with phrases like, "You are too big to cry. You've cried long enough, now stop it! If you don't stop crying, I will give you something to cry about. Don't come back in here until you can put on a happy face." In this way, children learn to deny and suppress any feelings of sadness because they know the parent will not accept those feelings from them.

All children develop a radar system to pick up signals from adults regarding what those adults want, need, and expect from them. They will conform to whatever false self is necessary to maintain a sense of acceptance and stability in the family system.

A false self is created as a cover-up from shame. If in the true self, I feel damaged and flawed, I need a false self, which appears to be acceptable. However, when a false self is adapted, I no longer exist as a genuine human being. It's as if the false self sneaks up on the true self (the one made in the image of God) and com-mits "soul murder" by stabbing the true self in the back. Therefore, I become separated from the true person, the unique individual that God intended for me to become. Shame has destroyed the lives of many in this way. In fact, most emotional illness happens as the byproduct of a shame-filled life lived in the false self.

In *Healing the Shame That Binds You*, John Bradshaw quotes Gershen Kaufman: "Shame is the effect which is the source of many complex and disturbing inner states: depression, alien-ation, self-doubt, isolating loneliness, paranoid and schizoid phenomena, compulsive disorders, splitting of the self, perfec-tionism, a deep sense of inferiority, inadequacy or failure, the so-called borderline conditions, and disorders of narcissism."[3]

This list of characteristics, created by Lane Ogden, will help you more clearly understand the difference between the true and false self:[4]

True Self	False Self
Real Self	Codependent Self
Genuine	Fake "As If" Personality
Spontaneous	Controlling
Loving	Fearful
Open and Giving	Closed and Withholding
Accepting of Others	Envious, Critical, Perfectionistic
Compassionate	Overly Conforming
Loves Unconditionally	Loves Conditionally
Feels Feelings	Denies or Hides Feelings
Assertive	Aggressive or Passive
Plays and Has Fun	Always Serious
Vulnerable	Falsely Strong
Trusting	Distrusting
Enjoys Being Nurtured	Avoids Being Nurtured

Symptoms of the False Self

When you become trapped in the false self, you lose touch with yourself and what you genuinely feel. Yet, you avoid intimate relationships because you're still aware that you are really "faking it." Uncertainty and insecurity brew inside, because you fear that someone will discover who you really are, and you will be rejected again. Your thought is, "If you know me, there is no way you could like me. Besides, I don't deserve to be loved."

Guilty thoughts pour through your mind and make you feel that somehow you have done something wrong. You may feel ashamed that part of you is so defective and bad that you have to hide yourself. You constantly guess at what normal is and try to act accordingly. After all, you think other people are normal, acceptable, and lovable.

You may have very poor self-esteem because you don't like yourself and feel disgusted with yourself since you know you're a phony. You probably do a lot of all-or-nothing, black-or-white thinking. For instance, you place everything in life on a mental report card as either an "A" or an "F." There is no middle ground or balance in your way of thinking. It is unlikely that you'll give yourself an "A," so you generally walk around feeling like a complete failure.

Ironically, you may show mercy toward other people, and often think mercy is your spiritual gift. But you judge yourself without mercy because you believe you can "never be good enough." Satan uses this area of "stinking thinking" to set up many lies in your belief system such as:

🐏 "You will never amount to anything."
🐏 "How could you dare to think someone could love you after all you've done wrong?"
🐏 "You are such a failure!"
🐏 "Why did you even bother to try? That made you look stupid in front of all those people."
🐏 "You should hang your head in shame. You can't do anything right."

In psychology, we call this "self-talk." But God's Word pointed out long ago that our thoughts produce our feelings: "For as [s]he thinks in [her] heart, so is [s]he" (Proverbs 23:7, NKJV). Satan certainly knows this, and he works hard to keep us in bondage to the many lies of self-defeat.

In the false self, your boundaries get tangled up or merged with the boundaries of others. Some of my clients don't even know what a boundary is, let alone that they might be allowed to establish one. This type of person is like a house with open spaces where doors and windows were never installed, leaving the interior vulnerable to robbery and vandalism. Individuality is not allowed in enmeshed relationships. Everybody knows everybody else's business. No one uses the word "no."

Foreign Emotions

Picture yourself as the parent of a six-year-old child. You allow your child to go out to play with neighborhood children after school one day. Before too long, you hear a scream and recognize it as the voice of your child in pain. You race outside to find the neighborhood bully has your child's arm twisted behind her back and has buried her face in the grass and dirt.

What is your first emotion? Anger! The Bible calls this "righteous indignation." And why would you be angry that someone was hurting your child? The answer is because you love that child and want to protect her. So the fuel that drives you to be angry enough to rescue your child from the bully is love. Love can actually motivate us to be angry.

However, people who live in their false self often find it difficult to express genuine thoughts and feelings because they have become so disconnected from their true self. So, when I hear a client express emotions like fear or anger, I want to stand up and cheer. It means that we are making progress. Those clients are finally getting back in touch with their true self. And as they start to feel angry about the abuse or neglect they have suffered, they learn to value themselves. For some, it is the first time they have felt important enough to be angry about the abuse they have suffered.

CONSEQUENCES

At some point, all of the shame, guilt, abusive self-talk, broken boundaries, and fear of intimacy become extremely painful if you live in your false self. So, you begin searching for a way to fill the hurting void inside. Instead of turning to a relationship with God, you may seek a form of anesthesia—your "drug of choice"—to numb some of the pain.

You may become involved in compulsive behaviors to try and break the confusing tension you feel. Those behaviors involve striving for perfection, overeating, starving, throwing up, exercising, spending money, getting involved in relationships, having sex, drinking, drugging, over analyzing, or over spiritualizing. But the fix won't last long, and then you're back to hurting again—often filled with more shame for how you tried to avoid your pain in the first place. Yet, unresolved shame will force you to regularly find another "fix."

Someone said insanity—like any addictive behavior—is doing the same thing over and over again and expecting different results. Truth is, you are never permanently trapped. You may feel that way, but feelings are very often based on untrue thoughts and beliefs. Remember that Satan wants to keep everyone in bondage to lies so that he can have control.

Isaiah 61:1-3 reveals the truth of God's plan for you through Christ: "He has sent me to bind up the brokenhearted, to proclaim freedom for the captives and release from darkness for the prisoners, to comfort all who mourn, and to provide for those who grieve—to bestow on them a crown of beauty instead of ashes, the oil of gladness instead of mourning, and a garment of praise instead of a spirit of despair. They will be called oaks of righteousness, a planting of the LORD for the display of his splendor."

Do you long to walk in light and not darkness, to be released from the prison of the past and your cruel self-talk? What a blessing to know that God offers comfort for grief, beauty in exchange for trash, gladness in place of wailing, and a delightful covering of praise instead of the heartbreak of despair.

God's Master Plan

There have been many times in my life when I have felt so wounded by the words or actions of others. It is often difficult to understand why things happen. One thing I have learned is that God knows what to do with my pain. I can look back with hindsight and see how God has used the circumstances of my past to make me dependent on Him, and to help me encourage others.

We live in a fallen and sinful world full of selfish, hurting people. But once abuse has occurred, it's as if God rushes in to confiscate the evil and confront the perpetrator: "You meant this to harm my child, but I will win a victory by using even the deepest of wounds to bring glory and honor to My name." In your journey to reconcile the abuses and sins of your past, know that God is working on your behalf!

Even in my darkest years of depression, spring always offered me encouragement of hope for new life, as I watched tiny green shoots struggle up through the dark soil where they had been dormant and cold—forgotten all winter. To encourage means to put courage into the life of someone else. I want to encourage you today that a new spring is coming into your life. Don't struggle. Have courage that God is in control. None of my flowers are working hard to grow. They are just relaxing outside in the warm sunshine and cool rains, and it becomes a natural process for growth to be produced. Soon, they will rise up to produce a beautiful showing of gloriously colored flowers.

In the same way, you don't have to worry about producing anything. It is the job of the Holy Spirit who lives in you to produce the fruit. Just pray right now and tell God that you are simply *available* for whatever He desires to do in your life. In the fertile soil of your availability, God is planting a precious seed of anticipation and hope for the future!

Part 2:

~

*The Hidden Places
of Shame*

~

four

The Inauthentic Church: Genuine Folks Not Accepted

Create in me a pure heart, O God,
and renew a steadfast spirit within me.
Do not cast me from your presence
or take your Holy Spirit from me.
Restore to me the joy of your salvation.
Psalm 51:10-12

I still remember the Saturday nights of my childhood as dreadful because it meant sleeping in those awful pink sponge rollers in order to have pretty curls for church. On Sunday morning, my mother set out our polished shoes and crisply starched clothes. Then, sometime during the drive to church, my mother would dampen a tissue to wipe one last spot from our little faces. (To this day, I remain convinced that a mother's spit is stronger than Formula 409 and can take the chrome off a bumper if necessary.) Upon arrival, we marched in and greeted everyone with our biggest Sunday smiles.

"And how are you this morning?" some dear old saint would croon.

"I am fine, thank you," was the only acceptable and expected response. And so we made our way to the second pew from the front, on the right side of the auditorium, and there we sat—looking like the perfect all-American family. In addition, my mother played the piano and my father served as the head deacon Sunday after Sunday for the first eighteen years of my life.

Outward appearances were of great importance at our church. The more stoic a person was, the more godly he or she must be. If you were struggling with emotional pain, you obviously needed a longer quiet time and more prayer. When I announced at age fifteen that I wanted to be a Christian counselor, I was promptly told there was no such thing.

"That psychology stuff is just a bunch of worldly nonsense!" the church folks declared. Vulnerability was not encouraged, so we all stuffed our feelings and came up with great motivational phrases like "Praise the Lord anyhow."

Have you ever played that game at church where people ask questions and they seem to show concern or interest, but you know there is only one acceptable answer? It usually goes something like this: You enter the church and walk down the hall to your Sunday school class as you pass the pastor in the hall.

"Well good Lord's day to you, Mary! How are you today?" he asks.

"Just fine, Pastor," you reply. "Can't wait to hear your sermon this morning." A minute later, you step into the restroom and a gal from your class asks about your kids.

"Is Tommy enjoying the seventh grade?" she inquires.

"Thank you for asking," you respond. "The kids are all great, and Tommy really likes his new school." After the Sunday school class dismisses, you slip into the sanctuary and take a seat next to a lady who immediately leans over to ask about your husband.

"We sure do miss him when he's not here," she whispers. With a faint smile you assure her that he'll be back in church next Sunday for sure. By then, he should be over the flu that's been going around. With that, you sit back in your seat, exhausted from the charade. You have difficulty listening to the pastor because your mind is overwhelmed by what's really going on in your home.

For instance, you wish you could have told him that you feel so depressed you can't see straight—that you think if life gets any more overwhelming, you don't know how you'll handle it. You want to ask if he could refer your family to a good counselor, but any of the above responses would blow your cover as a joyful Christian.

As for the woman you met in the restroom, you didn't tell her the truth either. Tommy hates seventh grade and is failing three subjects in the first grading session. He has a smart mouth and a defiant attitude, but you can't say that, because to admit Tommy's problems might reveal that you aren't "Suzy Sunshine" or the perfect mother after all.

And boy did that last question from the lady sharing your pew zing you in the heart. So where does she get off calling your husband "sweet"? Let her live with him for one day, and see if she wants him back in church! Furthermore, he does not have the flu. He's home nursing another hangover. He didn't even get home until 4 A.M. today.

This concludes the first round of "Fake it for the Brethren." You are worn out with covering everything up and wonder how you'll make it to your car without having to play the game all over again. You only hope you have the energy to fake it again without collapsing into tears.

Jesus confronted this very problem of "faking it" with the Pharisees of His day. He gave a word picture of their spiritual charade as being "like white-washed tombs full of dead men's bones." Picture a beautiful cemetery with rolling green lawns. On a prominent hill, a large white tomb has been freshly painted and stands as a glorious testimony to the life of the elite man who is buried there.

The peaceful surroundings make you want to sit quietly for a while. But, wait. What's that horrible stench? The odor gets so strong it overwhelms you and begins to burn your nose as you breathe. Something around here must be rotten! Upon closer inspection of this tomb, you feel sickened more. There in full view lies the decaying corpse! A wave of nausea hits, and you sprint from that ghastly scene. Suddenly the place that only moments ago seemed so peaceful has become a place of repulsion.

When we "play church" and pretend to "have it all together" spiritually, we may look great on the outside with our Sunday rituals, Sunday clothes, and Sunday faces. But our hearts prove that we are phony and full of rotten arrogance and pride.

Sadly, our fake perfection creates an atmosphere where only people who fit into our mold of Christianity are accepted. This performance makes others feel that there is no place for them at church if they admit that they are hurting and need help. So, in order to conform, some put on a mask, too. They join the charade, all the while dying a little more on the inside.

I remember suggesting church attendance to one of my clients, thinking it would give her some much-needed guidance. She promptly refused and told me that she already felt like a failure. Why would she want to go to a church where the people would make her feel even worse about herself?

The problem certainly isn't with God. Rather, the problem is that the churches are full of people who struggle with their own level of sin and dysfunction. Though designed to be a wonderful place where we freely gather to worship God, learn more about Him, and fellowship as a body of believers, the church—like a family—can be dysfunctional.

I know there are many dynamic and sincere churches ministering to the needs of those who are hurting. But no matter how spiritual, those church folks are still humans in need of God's grace, too. Nevertheless, it is the prayer of my heart that churches would become a place of shelter and guidance for those in need.

To admit that we have needs is not an admission of weakness, it's a confession of our humanity. We all have needs . . . that's the way God made us . . . and to admit that we have needs is not only truthful, it's beneficial.

Unfortunately, the reluctance to admit we have needs is often conveyed predominantly in Christian circles. We often succumb to a subtle but erroneous teaching that the more "mature" we become in Christ, the fewer needs we have and the less we need each other. Which, if taken to an extreme, produces a self-reliant, self-sufficient, egotistical, obnoxious, spiritual "maverick." [1]

Church Masks

Have you ever noticed how stressed out your family can get on Sunday mornings while getting ready for church? Many people tell me that if they are going to have a fight with their spouse, it will usually be on the way to church on Sunday morning. We rush through the church doors, all harried from the morning's preparation, take a deep breath, then put on our church mask. This mask gives us a safe place to hide from others. It presents a false front that shows we have it all together spiritually, that there are no doubts or struggles in our family.

Often, it seems we go into church feeling that we are not allowed to be authentic about who we really are, what we've been through in the past, and what our needs are now. If we cannot feel loved, safe, and accepted within the church, then where else can we possibly go for the kind of acceptance the church was designed to offer? In many churches there seems to be an unspoken set of rules as to how we must present ourselves.

For instance, to be a mature believer means that when tragedy strikes, we should have an immediate peace about it. What most people experience after a tragedy is shock, not peace. Shock is a system of denial that for a time holds back the reality and depth of our pain in order to allow us to cope with the immediate situation. If we push on people the idea that a strong Christian can only feel peace, then we set them up to stuff their feelings—to hide their anger and confusion.

I once counseled a woman who was losing her husband to cancer. She was only twenty-eight years old when he died and left her two toddlers. The week after the funeral, she came in all smiles and told me how much "immediate peace" she had at his deathbed and how proud she was that she didn't cry at the funeral. She then skipped therapy for the next six months. By the time she got in touch with her grief and anger, those stuffed feelings had festered enough to produce an acute case of depression.

Just as a broken bone would need medical attention, time to heal, and possible physical therapy for recovery, so too we must allow time for the healing of broken hearts and broken lives. Jesus came to "bind up the brokenhearted." If there were no wounds, He wouldn't be offering a cast or splint. It is the healing grace of His love that can bind our deepest wounds.

I have also counseled women with the exact opposite response to crisis. This type of woman spews anger, resentment, and frustration with God as she struggles through a divorce or the loss of a child. Church folks may tell her to be stronger and trust God in order to find peace and joy.

But, I can't see Jesus saying that to anyone. Why? Well, the Bible says "Jesus wept" (John 11:35). And Isaiah 53:3 declares, "He was a man of sorrows, and familiar with suffering." Our calling is not to be conformed to the image of the church—which is made up of a group of human beings—but rather to be conformed to the image of Christ.

> Lack of peace does not mean lack of conviction of faith. People in pain do not need sermons on peace. They need love and care and assistance through the healing process. Remember, faith in God will produce

a peace that will go beyond all understanding. It probably won't be an instant peace, but it will be a real peace.[2]

There have been times in my life when I have dared to share my inner pain, and someone immediately quotes Romans 8:28: "and we know that in all things God works for the good of those who love him, who have been called according to his purpose."

Don't get me wrong. I love that verse, and it does offer me hope. But when I am overwhelmed with pain, it takes time for me to find comfort in that Scripture. Sometimes when I hurt, I have difficulty praising God. In my human frailty I admit that I am much more prone to silently scream "Why?!?" I need the freedom to tell someone that I don't understand the ways of God, that I would not choose this path if God had checked with me for advice first, and that I don't particularly like the current situation.

When I share my doubts and my heartache, I need to be met with a safe and loving response of concern for my pain instead of criticism for my lack of faith. Reproof only adds to my shameful thoughts like believing that I am lacking something, that I am weak spiritually or just not good enough. Reproof confirms my unhealthy belief that other people are more godly, stronger, or more spiritual than I am.

Furthermore, when I am hurt, confused, or needy, the last thing I need to hear is, "You shouldn't feel that way. Take it to the cross. Maybe you need to spend more time in prayer because your faith seems weak." A much more helpful response, especially for those of us who struggle with shame, would involve getting a reassuring hug and confirmation that my feelings about the current situation are not "right or wrong." They are simply my feelings.

When someone shows me this kind of compassion, comfort, and concern, it gives me the strength to search for the truth of God's Word. It also reinforces the solace of His love because it is being modeled for me through the loving actions of another person. Then, I am more likely to have a change of my beliefs and feelings.

But if I deny the emotions and pretend that everything in my life is just great because I am a Christian, then I become full of resentment and bitterness over my unexpressed and unmet needs. I feel compelled to continue the charade of pretending to be "Super Christian."

> At long last, pastors and congregations alike have stopped whispering and started addressing the secret struggles that plague many, if not most families. Rather than pounding pulpits and demanding instant change, we have discovered that dysfunctional families are often in the church, and that recovery takes time and is a painful process and, in fact, that the process cannot be accelerated by cramming more and more convicting Scriptures down the throat of the abandoned or the abused. Guilt and shame are not friends of the grace that prompts inner healing.[3]

Unexpected Wounds

There is a major difference between being wounded by people in the world's system and being wounded by people in the church or in Christian ministry. When people in the world let us down, criticize us, gossip behind our backs, slander us to others, or hurt us in any way, we can say to ourselves, "That was painful, but I am not surprised. The people who just hurt me have no moral compass, so I expected them to be concerned with their own advancement over the needs of others."

But when we are wounded in the church, in a ministry, by a Christian organization, or a Christian friend, it is twice as painful. I've heard people say, "I expected the world to run over me, but I thought this would be a safe place where we cared for the needs of others."

However surprising, spiritual leaders need to know that giving a task to someone who is already swamped may contribute to that person's dysfunction and spiritual defeat. For instance, if the leader repeatedly recruits someone because he or she is hyper vigilant, people pleasing, and compulsive, this pattern can be a venomous poison that will burn out and damage the volunteer.

Remember this: Shame-driven Christians look the same as Spirit-driven Christians. The difference? The shame-driven Christian uses human effort versus the power of the Holy Spirit to accomplish goals. When asked to serve, this person feels burdened and thinks, "What *should* I do?" or "What is *expected* of me?" On the other hand, the Spirit-driven Christian asks, "What does God want to accomplish through me?" Shame-driven volunteers end up exhausted rather than empowered by their decision to serve.

I've counseled many women who have become disillusioned and left the church because they believed they could trust all church leaders. In response, I always explain the importance of regarding church leaders as real people with real problems. Though in a position of authority, church leaders face the same daily temptations we all face. So, no matter how godly a pastor is, we must not put that person on a pedestal.

In addition, if we put our faith in a leader instead of God, then we seem to think God has failed when the leader fails. We must remember that just because a person does not have pure faith, that doesn't mean the object of faith is also imperfect.

Yes, pastors of both small churches and large national ministries have manipulated, controlled, cheated, and molested. But instead of turning away from God because of the failures of mortals, we need to realize that these people represent the exception to the rule. Their sin shows us how vulnerable we all are, and how much we each need to grow in our faith and trust in God.

The Letter of the Law

When I was a teenager, the girls in the youth group had a saying that went like this: "We don't drink, dance, smoke, or chew, and we don't go with the boys who do." In the same way, some churches have lists of unspoken or spoken rules that members are expected to follow.

This is called legalism, and it has damaged the hearts of many because it leaves no room for God's grace. Legalism sets us up to think in an unhealthy, all-or-nothing, black-or-white way. There is no middle ground or gray area in this form of thinking.

Perfectionism is one of the key features of legalism. But classic legalism also involves stuffing your feelings unless they are positive. People caught in a legalistic approach to God live by the idea that they must work in order to gain His love and approval. Yet, when we believe we have to work to please God, we are actually trying to be in control. We forget Philippians 1:6: "Being confident of this, that he who began a good work in you will carry it on to completion until the day of Jesus Christ."

When you are able to keep the rules, it's easy to become prideful of your accomplishments and critical of the failure of others. And why not be critical? Criticizing others keeps the focus off you—where you need to be growing and changing. Some grow weary of aiming at perfection and failing, so they rebel against God and the church. Others continue trying to conform to the rules, not necessarily out of strength, but out of weakness, insecurity, or fear.

"What a freedom when my heart received the truth that God loved me in my humanity," one of my clients once shared. "I had always known He loved the unsaved unto Himself. But, I'd been indoctrinated that there was no excuse for human weakness for the believer. I've learned that my guilt is just a mirror of my humanity, and my humanity just an offering to the Lord. He receives and discards my guilt and my shame and then loves me in my humanity.

"I fought with God for ten years before He could tear apart my tarnished view of Him; before I could view the same Scriptures from a truthful and liberated point of view rather than a rigid point of view. I still struggle as all humans do, but the battle to embrace the truth of God's love for me was worth every step of the way, and I know it can bring you freedom too."

A CRITICAL SPIRIT

Matthew 7:1-5 reports Jesus' perspective on judging others: "Don't judge other people. Why are you so busy with your tweezers trying to get a speck of sawdust out of someone else's eye when you have a telephone pole sticking out of your own eye?" (That's my paraphrase.) Clearly, Jesus wants us to deal with our own issues before we dare to point out what someone else should be working on!

Plus, being critical sets us up to have a spirit of pride because we view ourselves as better than others. Have you noticed how critical people often lack warmth? There is nothing about the critical person that is inviting or that promotes vulnerability. Sure enough, it's as if judgmental people are so busy criticizing that they don't have time to demonstrate God's grace, kindness, and sweetness.

We need to remember when we were in sin, and how God pursued us with His great love to save us out of the darkness of that sin. Romans 2:4 tells us that it is the goodness and kindness of God that brings us to a place of repentance—not the judgments of others. And even God resists chasing us around with a spiritual baseball bat, hitting us over the head each time we make a mistake.

In the Garden of Eden, on the day when Adam and Eve first disobeyed God, God knew exactly what they had done. He had watched their every move, had known each thought as they calculated their choice to sin. And yet, God did not reject them. He could have gotten angry the moment they sinned and hurled a big lightning bolt down to strike them, or started a fire and burned up the whole Garden. Instead, God came to the Garden that evening *exactly* as He had done every night before.

He entered graciously because He wanted to continue His relationship with them. Certainly He was a brokenhearted Father because of their choice to disobey, but He was already planning a way to reconcile and restore His relationship to all mankind through the death and resurrection of His only Son, Jesus Christ.

REMEMBER YOUR ROOTS

In Wichita, Kansas, I had the privilege of being treated by Dr. Jeanine Cobb, a wonderful OB-GYN. She understands PMS and has gone through three C-section births of her own. Furthermore, before she became a doctor, she worked as an OB nurse for twelve years, which gave her valuable firsthand exposure to how much patients appreciate TLC.

When she completed her medical school residency, she remembered her roots and continued developing her bedside manner. And it shows. For instance, as the staff prepped me for a C-section, they had a few problems with the epidural. The first one caused painful spasms in my back. So they started over. The second attempt worked, but by the time I reached the operating table, I felt nauseated and started vomiting.

Instead of calling for a nurse, Dr. Cobb quickly got some cold, wet washcloths. After giving one to my mother, the two gently bathed my face until I could calm down enough for her to deliver Christian.

I've worked with a lot of doctors during my career, but I've never seen anyone as humble as she — and I told her so shortly thereafter. On that difficult delivery day, I saw her compassion and her great servant's heart as she performed the small acts of kindness. She saw a need in my life, and she immediately responded to it. That meant so much to me.

Clearly, Dr. Cobb remembers her days as a nurse, and she has not forgotten the three C-section births she endured. When we remember where we have come from, we are much more likely to express grace and kindness to others.

WHO ARE WE TO JUDGE?

Truth be told, if we got what we deserved, we would be sentenced to death and hell. We all owe a debt we can never pay. Yet, in His great mercy God paid a debt He did not owe through the death, burial, and resurrection of His Son. Except for God's amazing grace, we would all have died in our sins. When I remember this truth, I realize that I have no room to judge someone else.

The Bible shows that God consistently uses imperfect men and women to accomplish His will. Sometimes, He calls the least likely characters to accomplish great things in His name. Second Corinthians 4:7 sums up the idea well: "But we have this treasure in jars of clay to show that this all-surpassing power is from God and not from us."

God chooses to dwell in broken vessels so that all the glory goes to Him and not to us. His light is able to shine the brightest through the cracks! When I remember how much God has forgiven me, when I know that I am a defective vessel in which God graciously chooses to dwell, then I know that I have no right to be critical of others.

IT COULD BE ME

Recently, I visited a crowded church, and my jaw dropped when the pastor announced that he was a latent homosexual. You could hear people gasp! I looked around to see if anyone had gotten up to leave. He continued, saying, "I am also a latent murderer, a latent adulterer, a latent pornographer, a latent alcoholic, and a latent thief. You name the sin, and I am capable of it. So are you."

That certainly takes the wind out of my sails! In my religious pride, I want to believe that I am somehow elevated above certain sins, but in truth I must agree with the pastor.

Charles Wesley, that great founder of the Methodist church, once watched a man get hauled off to the gallows. With a broken heart for that criminal, he said, "There but for the grace of God goes Charles Wesley." It takes maturity to admit that, if left to our own devices, we are all capable of great falls. However, if we never climb up onto a pedestal in the first place, if we never become prideful and think we have "arrived," if we remain authentic and aware of who we truly are, then we will be living the life of humility God desires. Then, and only then, will people be drawn to us to share who they really are deep inside—how they hurt and what their needs are—because they will see in us a place of safety for being real.

A Shaming Faith?

Linda stood in the packed sanctuary with her eyes closed while the woman on stage prayed: "I see someone with severe back pain. You have struggled with this for many years and right now God is healing the discs in your spine. One of you is struggling with a failing marriage, and even now God is joining that relationship back together. There is a woman here who has suffered with depression for many years. . . . " Linda's heart began to pound in her chest!

"Surely she is talking to me!" Linda thought.

"Right now God is flooding you with great joy and healing," the speaker added. The service continued for another hour, but all Linda could do was stand and weep.

"This is it," she decided. "I am finally healed!"

The next week, Linda wanted to prove to God that she really had faith in receiving her healing, so she threw away her anti-depressant medications without consulting her doctor. Shortly thereafter, Linda felt frustrated with herself when she again felt depressed. She started having trouble getting out of bed and was easily irritated with her children. Finally, she called her pastor and told him she was certain that message of healing was intended for her.

"Why isn't it working?" she asked. "What could possibly be wrong?" The pastor's response cut through her heart like an icy dagger.

"It's pretty clear to me that you just didn't have enough faith to receive your healing, Linda. God was there to heal you," he explained, "but you must not have trusted that He would."

After the conversation ended, Linda turned out the lights in her room and crawled into bed. Shameful thoughts began to flood her mind: "This is my fault again. I can never get it right. I've wasted my whole life and ruined the lives of my husband and children. They don't deserve the torture of having me in their lives. Something is wrong with me, or I would be healed from this depression."

Doubt and fear began to fill her heart as she wondered, "Why was I born? Does God even hear my prayers or do they just bounce off the ceiling? He must not love me. If He loved me, He would heal me. How could God love such a messed up person anyway? Maybe there is sin in my life. Maybe I don't love God enough. This depression has to be my fault."

It took months of counseling for Linda to catch a glimpse of the truth. Until then, she believed the lie that says, "If you only have enough faith, you can move the hand of God to heal you or someone you love." When we hold onto this lie, our guilt and anger begin to build a barrier between us and God. Linda had to accept that God is God, and even when we don't understand the reasons—or even if we don't like His choices one bit—He is still the one in control.

We need to remember that God does not heal everyone. You may have incredible faith, but if God has a different plan for your life, you will not be healed. Perhaps God sees that healing might actually lead us away from Him instead of closer to Him.

I've reflected on this concept many times when confronted with my own struggles and those struggles my clients face. I trust completely that God has the power to heal, and yet I have never seen Him instantly and miraculously heal the emotional pain of a single client. It would be similar to instantly having the body of a bodybuilder. We would have no appreciation of the hard work it took to get those muscles, and we would have no training in how to maintain the muscle strength.

God is in the business of growing us up into maturity. Maturing is a process. We learn as we walk through our pain. We mature and gain depth in areas where we never would have grown if we had not suffered. I often do not enjoy the maturing process. At times, I have been known to angrily resist it. Yet, I am thankful that God holds my hand and guides me tenderly through. He does this in order to make me more like Him and to guide me to a place where I can offer comfort to others in similar situations.

Have you ever wondered what your life would be like if God had answered "yes" to each of your prayer requests? Think about that for a minute. It's a scary thought for me. I would have married the wrong person, would have gotten a new job when the current one got tough, and would have never lived in Texas or Kansas. The bottom line is, I would have prayed away all the suffering in my life.

Part of that sounds good to me, but I realize with hindsight that a "yes" God would have caused me to become a shallow, insensitive individual. I'm glad that God sees the big picture, and knows when to say "yes," "no," and "wait."

CLIQUE MEMBERSHIPS
I answered the phone and heard my friend Beverly say, "Are you busy right now?" I knew immediately from the tremble in her voice that she had been crying.

"Of course I'm not busy. Are you having a bad day?" I asked. The sobbing started again, and it took a few minutes to get the whole story. I knew Beverly's husband had been transferred to a new job in another state just three months earlier. But I had no specific idea of why she was so upset.

"I'm never going to fit in here," she cried. "We've been going to the same church since we arrived here, and no one speaks to me. We go to Sunday school, but the women seem to already have their little cliques of friends. I feel as though I would be interrupting or barging into their exclusive group if I approach them, so I just sit in the back of the room and wait for class to start. Is there something wrong with me? I thought Christians were supposed to be warm and kind. Maybe we should go to another church."

One of the ways women often hurt each other in church is by forming cliques. To the outside observer, it appears that these women have joined together in a tight circle with their backs to the rest of the world. Consequently, women who are not accepted by these groups feel rejected, isolated, or somehow flawed. It is uncomfortable to feel uninvited, left out, or unable to penetrate into the group.

Let's face it, we all want to be part of a group—to feel like we belong. Most women don't intentionally try to leave others out. Rather, cliques usually form because of our own insecurities. We find a group where we feel safe and then we cling together without even realizing that we are leaving out others who are just as needy of acceptance and safety as we are.

If you are involved in a church group, examine your own situation. Would other women feel left out if they saw you with your close groups of church buddies? Do you pay attention and reach out to new people? Friends are a blessing, and you have six other days of the week to spend time together. Try to be sensitive to the needs of others so you can open up and invite other women to feel safe and accepted at church.

WATCH YOUR MOUTH

Back in the "good ole' days" of the 1960s, my brother and I used to roam freely through the streets and woods of Georgetown, Mississippi, population 300. Everyone knew our family. In fact, my grandfather owned the local general store and cotton gin. For reasons unknown to me now that I am a mother, we were allowed to carry firecrackers from the store in our pockets and stick matches to light them.

Being the only girl as well as the youngest in the group, I decided one afternoon to show off and impress my brother and cousins. We were standing at the entrance to the cotton gin when I pulled a match from my pocket and said, "I wonder if old cotton will burn?"

With that brilliant question, I struck a match against the metal wall and tossed it onto a floor covered in dried cotton scraps. As if gasoline had been poured out, the floor burst into flames. We were terrified! We quickly doused some burlap sacks in the nearby creek eventually putting out the fire. I'm thankful that I threw the match into a metal-walled room, or I would have burned down the entire building!

James 4:3-7 describes the tongue as a small part of the body which can do tremendous damage. It takes only a small spark to create a huge forest fire. We women (and I'm raising my hand too) tend to have a problem with gossip. We are created to be intimate in relationships. So, sharing a juicy tidbit of information creates a false feeling of intimacy between two women. I've even heard women gossip in the form of a prayer request! Are we creative or what?

Therefore, we must choose our words carefully and check out our motivation when talking about other people. Usually, the gossip gets back to the woman you are talking about, and she can be wounded even more deeply. We are called to build each other up, and gossip is a sneaky trick that Satan uses to tear us down and pull us apart.

In Sum

I wrote this chapter for two key reasons. First, if you have been shamed or otherwise rejected in the church, remember that you were hurt by people and not by God. Some of you have been wounded and judged for out-of-wedlock pregnancies, for marrying someone with a different faith or skin color, for getting a divorce or struggling with an addiction. God is the God of second chances. God is still here to offer you comfort, encouragement, and restoration.

You don't buy the first car you test drive when shopping for a new car. You take your time to research your decision. It is also helpful to visit several churches before prayerfully deciding on the one where you get the strongest sense that the members are living authentic Christ-like lives. Only loving and accepting people can offer you the safety and grace you need to learn more about a loving relationship with God.

Secondly, if this chapter has convicted you of being judgmental, legalistic, unsupportive of others, or phony for hiding behind a mask of self-righteousness, then I urge you to prayerfully determine that—with God's help—you want to change. Those changes start in our heart as we work through our own issues, allowing God to help us drop our guard and learn to be transparent and authentic.

God calls His church the "body of Christ." A body needs all of its parts functioning well together in order to live a healthy life. So too, the church needs each member of the body to support every other member so that God may receive the honor and glory. Let's work together to mature in faith so that we might create a safe church where people can be genuine and where the needs of those who are hurting can be met.

five

Addiction:
The Perfect Mask

The Spirit of the Sovereign LORD is on me,
    because the Lord has anointed me to preach
    good news to the poor;
He has sent me to bind up the brokenhearted,
    to proclaim freedom for the captives
    and release from darkness for the prisoners . . .
To comfort all who mourn,
and provide for those who grieve . . .
    to bestow on them a crown of beauty instead of ashes,
    the oil of gladness instead of mourning,
    and a garment of praise instead of a spirit of despair.
They will be called oaks of righteousness,
    a planting of the LORD for the display of his splendor.
        Isaiah 61:1-3

*W*endy grew up in a family that looked great from the outside. But on the inside, her family was quietly dysfunctional. First of all, her father was a very distant, passive man who did not know how to express emotions. So, Wendy grew up feeling emotionally abandoned by her father, believing the lie that something must be wrong with her that kept him from showing his love.

Secondly, Wendy's parents cast her in the role of the "people pleaser" early on. To live up to this expectation, Wendy tried to make everyone in the family system feel better by aiming at perfection. She truly believed that if she hit perfection, she would somehow earn the right to be loved.

Thirdly, her family attended church every time the doors were open, but this church was full of legalistic rules. Expressing anger was taboo both at church and at home. So Wendy stuffed anything that came close to a negative emotion. Expressing anger would surely bring with it the shame of being found unacceptable. Over time, the anger-turned-inward soon began to show itself in forms of childhood depression. No one knew what to do with depression in those days, so her parents ignored it in hopes that it was just a stage she was going through. Yet the drive to be perfect continued.

By the time Wendy left home for college, the undiagnosed depression had become overwhelming. At times she hurt so much, she prayed that God would let her die. She struggled in her relationship with God because she saw Him in relationship to her earthly father. In this way, she incorrectly believed she had to work harder to earn His approval. However, Wendy grew weary of working harder. Spending time in God's Word eventually felt like a chore instead of a sweet time of fellowship that she wanted to enjoy. She knew lots of rules, but had no understanding of God's grace.

During her freshman year, some friends offered her a drink. Wendy had grown up in a home where no one drank alcohol, and she knew that getting drunk was wrong. But her emotional pain outweighed the rules, and she accepted the cheap wine. Immediately, she felt a calm. When she drank more, she felt even better because she forgot about the pain of her depression.

Wendy had no way of knowing that when she took that first drink it would lead her into alcoholism. She had no way of knowing that the liquid she had found to ease her pain would lead her into years of addiction filled with shameful regrets over her words, actions, and behaviors. All she knew was that when she drank, she didn't hurt as much. The alcohol numbed her painful emotions for a while.

By the time Wendy was twenty-four, she had excelled in her career. Everything about her continued to look great from the outside. People admired the way she was so driven toward success. No one realized that she often escaped the pain of her depression and perfectionism by getting drunk alone. The alcohol binges numbed her tortured mind for a few hours, but the anger and hatred she felt toward herself the next day for "failing again" seemed to start the cycle of addiction and self-abusive behavior all over again.

"What's wrong with me?" she sadly wondered. "Why can't I be normal and get my life together like everyone else? Why won't God make this all go away? I try so hard, but nothing ever works. I never get it right. I wish I had never been born."

You Are What You Think

Your brain is like a human tape recorder that records 24/7. All your life, you have been recording messages from other people, the church, and even the media. You don't even have to be aware that the recording session is taking place. Once the message is put in place, you don't need to push the "play" button in order to hear the message, it just plays automatically. That explains why shame-filled people don't need another person around in order to be verbally abused. We are really good at doing it to ourselves. In fact, some of us say things to ourselves that are so cruel we would never dare to say them out loud to someone else!

However, the Bible is very clear about the results of shaming self-talk. Proverbs 23:7 (NKJV) teaches, "For as he thinks in his heart, so *is* he." Therefore, whatever we say to ourselves has a definite impact on how we feel about ourselves.

For example, I have a problem of locking my keys in the car at least once a year. It's strange how you know the keys are still in the car before the door even slams shut, but there is nothing you can do about it. When my husband David and I lived in Dallas, it cost forty dollars to have a locksmith come out to unlock a car. Thank goodness it only costs twenty-eight dollars in Wichita!

After I made this mistake, I would stand in the parking lot, gaze at my keys inside the car, and start talking to myself: "Cynthia, you are a stupid idiot! Why can't you pay attention to your keys? This is so embarrassing. You don't have the money to pay for this. Nobody else does this with their keys. When will you ever get it right?"

By the time I got through this whole session of criticizing myself, the keys were still locked in the car. The only thing that changed was my emotional state. I felt anxious and like a complete failure.

Through the years, I've learned to be more gracious to myself. Now I look at the keys dangling from the ignition and think, "I really don't like it when I lock my keys in the car. I'd better go call someone for help. Cynthia, welcome to the human race. You have just proven that you are a certified member again today."

With that changed attitude, I can get on with my day without verbally beating myself up. (By the way, I finally wised up and joined AAA, and they unlock my car for free!)

The Lie of Perfection

At some level, everyone feels inferior. Many of us spend most of our lives struggling with extreme feelings of inferiority, trying to overcome those feelings by being super-achievers. However, nothing we accomplish makes us feel better about ourselves, so we end up feeling depressed—finding little satisfaction or joy in life.

Perfectionists typically set unrealistically high standards they've never met and can't possibly meet. Yet, they hang on to these standards as if they were objects of worship. It's as if we say to ourselves, "If I can just be perfect, then I can put these feelings of inferiority to rest and accept myself." Or as Wendy thought, "If I can be perfect, everyone in my family will be happy, and my father will finally love me."

What exactly is perfectionism? Dr. David Burns offers this good definition:

> I do not mean the healthy pursuit of excellence by men and women who take genuine pleasure in striving to meet high standards. Without concern for quality, life would seem shallow and true accomplishments would be rare. . . . I am talking about . . . those whose standards are high beyond reach or reason, people who strain compulsively and unremittingly toward impossible goals and who measure their own worth entirely in terms of productivity and accomplishment. For these people, the drive to excel can only be self-defeating.[1]

Striving for perfection often comes at a great emotional price primarily because perfectionists tend to think in an all-or-nothing way. It's an "A" or an "F," a pass or a fail. With this approach, perfectionists are doomed from the start. They consistently set the highest standards for themselves because they worry that without that structure, they will not accomplish anything. Yet, perfectionists live with a deep fear of failure and often don't realize that striving for perfection actually sets them up to fail.

Consider two baseball players—"Paul the Perfectionist" and "Ed, the Player of Excellence." Both guys step up to bat one Saturday, and both strike out. Paul walks away from home plate and thinks, "You stupid idiot! You just struck out in front of all these people! You should have never played baseball in the first place!" Paul may as well hit himself over the head with the baseball bat a few times as well. After all, he has just beaten himself up verbally.

Ed, on the other hand, walks away from the plate and thinks, "I don't like it when I strike out. I wonder what I could do this week to improve my chances of hitting the ball next week?" He acknowledges that he did not practice last week, and that he wasn't keeping an eye on the pitcher because he was looking in the stands to see if his girlfriend was watching.

All week long, Paul grumbles to himself about what a terrible baseball player he is. He berates himself for not hitting the ball last Saturday. Meanwhile, Ed spends his week hitting for an hour each day, determined to keep his eye on the pitcher the next time he steps up to bat.

Who do you think has a better chance of hitting the ball at the next game? Ed, of course, because he used his mistake to improve—instead of berate—himself. Paul's game probably worsened because all he did was put himself down for not being the perfect baseball player. Furthermore, even if Paul hits a single this week and gets to first base, he won't be pleased with himself because he believes he should have hit a home run! If Ed gets a hit, he'll be pleased with himself knowing that his hard work toward improving has paid off.

When you make a mistake—as we all will—the best thing to do is learn from it. Criticizing yourself for making the mistake will not change it. But you *can* change how you will handle the same situation next time if you look at it graciously and determine what needs to change.

Women who believe the lie of perfectionism live with an irrational shame. For instance, they believe that if someone finds out about their failures, they will be considered a complete failure and even "damaged goods." Still, in order to feel safe, they wear a mask of perfection and seek to gain everyone's love and approval by trying to do everything right.

Most of us have a longing to love and be loved, and to move closer to God who is the source of love. Unfortunately, we can become tangled up in a false pursuit of that love when we seek to earn it by doing everything perfectly.

When we expect ourselves to be perfect, we become ashamed of our own needs—ashamed of our humanness. Shame is Satan's lie continued and one of his most powerful methods of destroying the person God created us to be. The lie of shame separates us from the life-flow of fellowship with God in the same way that severing an artery would separate us from the life-giving flow of blood in our body.

Shame inhibits our ability to allow the Holy Spirit to produce in us the healthy spiritual fruits of love, joy, and peace. Like Adam and Eve, we now feel a need to hide from the presence of God instead of running straight into His healing embrace.

Codependency

When I finished graduate school in 1986, I had never heard the word "codependent." Maybe it was mentioned one day while I was skipping class, but I doubt it. As a matter of fact, I was shocked the next year when I read Melody Beattie's best-selling book, *Codependent No More*. I thought for sure she had secretly followed me around and written a book about me without my permission!

Early research regarded codependents as enablers for alcoholics and drug addicts. For instance, consider this classic codependent relationship: the sober wife with an alcoholic husband. His cycle of addiction is obvious, but what about her? She too is in pain. And, although her addiction looks different, she shares her husband's search for pain relief. However, identifying her anesthetic is more difficult because it doesn't come in a bottle. She may even be unaware of her method of avoiding pain.

The painkiller of martyrdom can be very intoxicating. Many of us enjoy wallowing in it occasionally as we think, "Poor pitiful me. I work so hard to help others, only to get walked over every time. No one will ever know how much I sacrifice, but it's nothing really." Some Christians even appear to be noble in their martyrdom. They like to think that no woman has ever suffered more than they have in their dedication to take care of their drunken husband.

This type of woman denies her own pain and anger. After all, admitting her feelings would reduce the satisfaction and anesthesia of her martyrdom. Nursing her drunken husband, covering for his drunken episodes and hangovers, and cleaning up after he gets sick from drinking gives her a fleeting high of usefulness and achievement.

Who Are You Calling Codependent?

In my own life, being a good codependent showed itself in many ways. My self-worth was so low that I only felt lovable if other people loved me. It became my goal in life to gain everyone's love and approval. I would change my opinions and ideas in order to fit in with others. I could not tolerate conflict, so I would quickly take responsibility by apologizing, even when I was the victim and had done nothing wrong.

I believed I was responsible for other people's feelings, and that they were responsible for my feelings. If I was upset, lonely, or sad, it was someone else's fault. I had no idea what a boundary was. The words "no" and "stop" were not in my vocabulary.

If someone hurt me, I believed it must have been an accident, or that I somehow caused it. It was difficult for me to see that people might be manipulative or hurtful on purpose. If I believed that, I might have to tell them to stop. If I told them to stop, then they might abandon me, and I would be left with my greatest fear—rejection. I felt desperate to do anything in order to avoid abandonment. I denied that other people were causing me pain.

I also told myself that I was so kind because my spiritual gift was mercy. And I felt good about myself for being such a great caretaker for others. I developed radar for gathering "stray puppy" types and trying to rescue them by meeting all of their needs. Ironically, I was hypersensitive to the needs of others, but had no idea what I needed. When others hurt, I was there to comfort them. But when I hurt and felt depressed, I criticized myself for being weak.

During this time, my self-talk was very abusive. I once told a friend that I didn't need anyone around to criticize me when I made a mistake because I was the first person to nail myself to the wall. This self-talk revealed some of the loathing I felt toward myself. It also disclosed my unrealistic expectations of perfection—emotionally and otherwise.

My life never felt stable then. I felt high when someone told me how sweet I was and how much I helped him or her, and I felt extremely low when anyone pulled away from me. Life as a codependent was like one terrible roller coaster ride.

Despite all my personal problems, I kept searching for my knight in shining armor and hoped that, once found, he could make me feel complete. I joked that I always felt like a door-mat in relationships, and that the other person was wearing cleats. After that person had walked all over me, I would call back and say, "Could you try that again? I think you missed a spot over here on my heart." It took me a long time to know that if I was being treated like a doormat, it was because I lay down and wrote "welcome" on my forehead.

Codependency Characteristics

Codependents share many of the same traits. Commonly, they are driven by compulsions, and also struggle with addictions. Many of their behaviors are responses to the dysfunctional family they grew up in. They feel worthlessness and often act in childish ways. They make others responsible for their feelings, and feel that they are powerful enough to control the feelings of others.

Codependents are also very skilled in denial. They often worry about things they cannot change. (I was once accused of worrying about not having anything to worry about!) The life of a codependent may feel similar to a person being thrown into the ocean without knowing how to swim. Life would feel desperately out of control. The person would search frantically for something to hang onto as a lifejacket. There is a sense of magical thinking that if she finds whatever is lacking in her life, she will be happy, stable, and fulfilled. Codependency is a very painful way of life.

Understanding Addiction

When you are wounded emotionally, physically, or sexually during childhood, you are defenseless to take care of yourself. The hurt done toward you is like having an emotional wound on your heart. It's as if the hurts in your heart fester and form emotional puss wounds. Yet, we are often unaware of the root issues in our hearts. We are only aware that we are in tremendous pain. This pain can manifest itself through codependent relationships, addictive behaviors, depression, anxiety, and suicidal thoughts. Symptoms like these often motivate people to seek counseling.

I've had twelve root canals and two oral surgeries in my lifetime. That means if you've never had a root canal, you owe me a thank-you note for having yours for you! (Can you imagine how excited I get about going to the dentist?) I could have gone to the dentist with each abscessed tooth and simply asked him to shoot it full of Novocain. The Novocain would stop the pain, but the reprieve would only be temporary.

While I would have felt relief from the pain, the abscess would still be in there, and the infection would grow worse as I ignored it. Getting rid of the pain permanently—be it in your mouth or your heart—requires going through the uncomfortable process of removing the wound and the years of infection. Yet, we often treat our emotional pain with any anesthesia we can find.

Self-medicating painful thoughts and feelings is the main purpose of addictions. When emotional pain becomes unbearable, we often seek to find an instant mood alteration to ease it. Most associate drug and alcohol abuse with addiction because they create the most obvious life-damaging consequences.

But addictive behavior also includes emotional and process addictions. In other words, hurting people have "drugs of choice" to ease their pain. One person may use work in the same way that another uses food to escape and ignore feelings. However various the addictions, all are used to change current reality to make it bearable if only for a while.

Ultimately, addictions are self-defeating forms of abuse that make the addict do things she doesn't really want to do. Recall the words of apostle Paul in Romans 7:14-24: "I do not understand my own behavior; I do not act as I mean to, but I do the things I hate. Though the will to do what is good is in me, the power to do it is not; the good thing I want to do, I never do; the evil thing which I do not want—that is what I do."

People may be addicted to alcohol, narcotics, power, work, relationships, money, shopping, perfectionism, spiritualism, exercise, eating, throwing up, starving, fantasies, masturbation, sex, and an endless variety of things. At one point, I was actually addicted to negative emotions.

It seems strange that I became addicted to something painful instead of something that brings pleasure. Even though my sadness was negative, it was easier for me to manage it than to deal with the more painful emotions of anger and rage. I knew I could tolerate depression because it seemed safe and well known to me, but I feared anger because I had no idea how to express it.

I later learned that many women have been taught not to be angry. We are told that sweet Christian girls don't get angry, or that anger isn't ladylike. We fear losing our parents' love and experiencing the great shame of being unacceptable if we express our anger. However, by repressing the healthy emotion of anger, we grow up into adults who are unable to protect ourselves from abusive relationships or to set boundaries with others. Without anger, we don't know how to say "no." Women with no voice of anger are often set up to become victims of violence at the hand of abusers.

The Cycle Continues

When a person is excessively devoted to something or surrenders compulsively and habitually to something, that pathological devotion becomes an addiction. The presence of a psychological and physiological dependency on a substance, relationship, or behavior results in addiction. When a person would sacrifice family, job, economic security, and sanity for the sake of a substance, relationship, or behavior, addiction exists. When a destructive relationship to something becomes the central part of the person's life, when all else is sacrificed for the sake of that sick relationship, the person is said to be addicted.[2]

Addictions are usually multi-generational. A common scenario involves a sexually addicted father who molests his daughter. The daughter then tries to deal with the pain of incest through an eating disorder. She may rear a son who works to prove he is lovable through perfectionism and workaholism. That son will neglect his children. As a result, his son may turn to alcohol for comfort and his daughter—who is starved for male attention—may become codependent on male relationships. She will tolerate abuse instead of being alone.

The addiction may look different in every generation, but the reason is the same. People in pain seek ways to alter their mood instead of dealing with the painful issues.

Picture yourself standing at the top of a hill on a snowy winter day with nothing but open pasture in sight. You make a large snowball, then give it a swift push downhill. It immediately starts to grow in size as it gathers more and more snow. By the time it reaches the bottom of the long hill, it's out of control and larger than you ever could have imagined. Addiction has a snowball effect. It cycles around, gathers speed, and is soon more destructive than we ever could have envisioned.

The first step in the cycle of addiction involves suffering pain. It may be due to guilt and shame, loneliness, low self-esteem, perceived failure, or the painful damage of childhood abuse or neglect. To escape the pain, we search for some form of anesthesia. Once the effect of the "drug of choice" wears off, we are left in pain again. Only this time, the volume is turned up even louder on our pain because we have added to it the guilt and shame of our addictive behavior. As our pain increases, we are drawn back to the anesthesia to try to numb the pain again. Only each time we come down from the anesthesia, the lows get lower, but the highs don't get any higher.

For instance, a single woman sitting alone in her apartment may feel overwhelmed with loneliness. In her self-talk she thinks, "Of course no one is ever going to ask me out. I am overweight. If I weren't so fat, maybe some guy would pay attention to me. I am never going to get married. I will be alone for the rest of my life."

Eventually, these thoughts become so painful that she searches for an anesthesia to calm her pain. She orders an extra large pizza and eats it alone. Then she eats a bag of cookies for dessert. As she eats, her anxiety lowers, and she feels comforted.

But after she has eaten it all she feels panicked, and her stomach hurts. She knows that now she will gain even more weight!

When food is used as anesthesia, either obesity or bulimia becomes the consequence. The hateful self-talk leads to more shame and guilt as she tells herself that she should never have been born, that no one will ever love her, or that God must be sick of her and her struggles. She feels like a worthless mess. Soon, the pain builds and the cycle starts again as she returns to binge on food for comfort.

In 1987, I bought my first house in Plano, Texas. I was so excited to be a new homeowner. Unfortunately the yard had been neglected and was full of weeds. One Saturday, I spent the entire day pulling dandelions. It was a sweaty, backbreaking job. Yet, I was so proud of how clean it looked when I was finished.

About two weeks later, after a rainstorm, I noticed the yard was full of dandelions again. I had not known that a dandelion has a long underground root. So, I wasted my efforts by breaking the plant off at the surface and leaving the root system entrenched.

We often do that with our addictions. We may stop drinking cold turkey or limit our exercise to three times a week or cut up all of our credit cards, but if we do not deal with the root issues that are causing the pain, the addiction will pop right back up like the weeds in my yard.

Furthermore, we can swap addictions and then somehow convince ourselves that we have changed. Some alcoholics stop drinking and start smoking. Some bulimics stop purging only to start working out obsessively or abusing laxatives. A woman may break up with an abusive boyfriend and find herself spending her way into bankruptcy.

All addictions result from a lack of healthy esteem for oneself. You cannot love yourself the way God desires for you to and abuse yourself at the same time. For example, if an alcoholic loved herself, she wouldn't get drunk and feel sick with a hangover for days at a time. If the bulimic loved herself, she wouldn't gorge on large amounts of food and then force herself to throw up. If the workaholic loved herself, she wouldn't work eighty-hour weeks and drive herself toward burnout.

Our repeated sins of addiction are also based on ego and pride. We want control. We don't like the way God is handling this problem, or maybe we won't even wait to give Him a chance to handle it. We just know that we don't like it, or that it hurts too much. So, we try desperately to be god in our own life. But, whenever we try to be God, someone always gets hurt.

Addiction Is Idolatry

The first commandment is: "Thou shalt have no other gods before me." If you ask most Christians if they keep idols, they would say, "Well, of course I don't keep idols in my house! Are you kidding? There is no Buddha, golden calf, or other graven image in my home." But if you take a closer look at the power of addiction in someone's life, it is an idol.

According to the New Testament, idolatry happens anytime you put something or someone other than God in a position of control in your life (see 1 John 2:15-17). Whatever you spend time and energy obsessing about gets elevated to the level of becoming lord of your life. That's right. If your heart is controlled by bitterness and unforgiveness, alcohol, eating, exercise, working, an adulterous relationship, or even perfectionism and people pleasing, you have placed those things in a higher position than God.

Beauty for Ashes

This chapter opened with Wendy's story. Remember, she was the little girl who grew up in church, became depressed in that repressive environment, then eventually became an alcoholic to temporarily soothe her pain. She finally broke free from her addiction to alcohol through Christian counseling and the abundance of God's grace. With this support, she began replacing the lies she believed were the truth.

For instance, she learned that if her father did not love her, it wasn't because she was an unlovable person. His lack of love was about his own generational inheritance and not about her. She realized that she was not flawed and was, in fact, a lovable person. Wendy also learned to have truthful self-talk, and works to love and accept herself in the same loving way that God sees her. She knows life can be difficult, but she seeks help with her struggles and has gained strength by trusting in God to meet her needs.

If you grew up with unloving parents, please know that you were not responsible for their lack of affection and acceptance. Lack of love is never a child's fault. All children are lovable, wonderful creations of God. If parents are unloving it is usually because they were never loved by their own parents and don't know how to express emotions.

In Isaiah 61:3, God says He will "give us beauty for ashes." At first, I thought that meant God would take the dirt in our lives and create something beautiful out of it. Then, I compared dirt with ashes and realized that there are many differences.

For those of you who have smoked, lived with a smoker, or cleaned ashes out of a fireplace, you know that ashes can make a terrible mess. Ashes are what's left over after all that is useful is burned up. Ashes weigh less than dirt and can easily be blown around and scattered to create an even bigger mess.

In cleaning dirt, mud will usually dry so that it can be flaked off fabric or vacuumed out of carpet, but ashes only smear and make an even larger stain. The more you rub the ash, the more it spreads. Also, as a gardener, I know that dirt has a useful purpose. It is used to grow a seed and produce new life in fruit or flowers. To my knowledge, ashes are good for nothing except to be thrown into the garbage.

It's tempting to consider the messiness in our lives is like dirt, not ashes. If that were true, we could roll our wheelbarrows of dirt up to God, explain where it came from, and watch Him accept the dirt, using it to plant a beautiful garden.

That scenario would be nice. However, I envision crawling to God dragging buckets full of ashes. In this case I might say, "God, look at all of this ash. It has stained my clothes and my skin so deeply that I don't know how to wash it off. I don't know how to get rid of it. Can you please help me?"

"I've been waiting for you to come home," God would gently say. "I'm so glad you're here. I've missed you desperately, Little One. Let's see . . . It looks like you have a pile of ash that weighs 2,567 pounds. But over here, I have three billion pounds of grace to bury it in because where sin has increased, grace has increased all the more (see Romans 5:20). My dear child, you can never out-sin my love for you. Come closer and let Me remove the stains and damage of your past. Let Me purify your heart and take away the shame that has bound you. Allow My unconditional love for you to change your appearance from a life darkened with pain and shame, to a face that radiates the light of my joy and peace."

I am humbled to understand that only God's tender love can take the ash of my life—the failures, the repeated sins of addiction, the damaging relationships, the hateful words and actions—and transform them into something healthier, something that can bring glory and honor to His name.

six

*S*TOLEN PURITY:
THE BROKEN BOUNDARIE*S* OF *S*EXUALITY

Have mercy on me , O God, have mercy on me,
for in you my soul takes refuge.
I will take refuge in the shadow of your wings
until the disaster has passed.
I cry out to God Most High,
to God, who fulfills his purpose for me.
He sends from heaven and saves me,
rebuking those who hotly pursue me,
God sends his love and faithfulnes.

PSALM 57:1-3

After I tapped softly on the door of the hospital room, a female responded, "Come in." I pushed the door open and realized the room was completely dark except for a small ray of light coming through a corner of the closed curtains. In the dim light, I could barely make out the form of a woman curled up on the bed.

"Hi, Ann," I said quietly. "My name is Cynthia, and I am going to be your counselor." Suddenly, she rose and threw a box of tissue at me! I moved aside as it flew past my head.

"Get out of my room!" she screamed. "I saw you in the hall-way, and you look just like the blondes my first husband used to have affairs with. Get out of here now! I don't want you to be my therapist!"

To be perfectly honest, at that moment, I had no desire to be her therapist *or* to stay in that room! It was the first time one of my patients had ever thrown something at me or asked me to leave. I silently prayed for wisdom. As a counselor who didn't have all the answers, I often meditated on James 1:5: "If any of you lacks wisdom, he should ask God, who gives generously to all."

This was definitely one of those times when I needed a fresh supply of God's wisdom! Instead of dashing out the door, I flipped on the light switch and moved to sit down in a nearby chair. My heart pounded, and I hoped she didn't have anything else to throw at me.

"Ann, I can understand why you might want a different thera-pist. But right now, I am the only one available," I explained. "Let's make a deal. Today is Wednesday. Why don't we work together for the rest of the week? If by Monday you still want a new therapist, I'll transfer you to someone else."

She scowled, and I knew she was by no means thrilled with my idea. But she was also too desperate to wait until the next week to start her therapy. So, she agreed. It's hard to believe, but after leaving the hospital, Ann remained in outpatient ther-apy with me for five years. Sometimes God develops relation-ships in ways we can never imagine.

I soon learned that shortly after her fortieth birthday, Ann had been admitted to an inpatient treatment facility for holding a gun to her head and threatening to commit suicide. She had reached a place of such severe self-hatred and depression that she wanted to take her own life.

Ann had been the victim of sexual abuse and incest. For years she had flashbacks of the abuse and carried the guilt and shame of believing the abuse was somehow her fault—that she was horrible for feeling pleasure at times, and that she should have been able to stop it.

Her earliest childhood memory was of her uncle masturbating in the bed next to her when she was only four years old. He threatened to tell her mother that she had wet the bed and shamed her into believing it was her fault. Throughout childhood and adolescence, she would wake up to one of her older brothers masturbating her. They would then force her to engage in oral sex. All told, she was filled with the terror and damage of seven sexual abusers—uncles, cousins, two of her brothers, and her father.

Incest and sexual abuse damages victims down to the very soul of who they are. When Ann and I began the therapy process, she said every moment of her life had been contaminated by the sins of others. She was so ashamed and wounded that she saw no reason to continue living. She was filled with self-contempt.

For this reason, she had become addicted to compulsive overeating years earlier. This addiction helped numb her painful memories. Ann criticized herself constantly for her obesity, and yet the weight was a security that kept her safe from being sexually attractive. She used it to build a physical barrier of protection around her wounded heart—a barrier that she knew would protect her by keeping men away.

Ann also had to deal with the painful relationship she had with her mother, a woman who repeatedly told her, "I always wanted a pretty little girl with nice straight teeth and long, thick hair." The problem was that Ann had buckteeth and stringy, thin hair.

Her mother also used her in an emotionally incestuous way by constantly telling Ann about the details of her husband's extramarital affairs. Furthermore, Ann wondered why her mother had not rescued her from the abuse that had taken place under their same shared roof.

To heal, Ann needed to express her anger about the abuse and the abusers. She also needed to grieve her lost childhood and to accept God's grace to help her forgive the past. It was not easy. At times, we moved forward. Other times, we went backward. Her depression continued to be overwhelming, and she still wanted to die. But she courageously kept trying to move forward. Although I acted as her guide, God used Ann to teach me many lessons about His grace and His healing power of forgiveness.

Now, fifteen years after we started, Ann is the grandmother of six. Like everyone, she has good days as well as bad. Yet, she lives in the truth now—she understands that the abuse was not her fault. With this knowledge, she has grown to love and accept herself as the precious woman God intended her to be. She also lost weight and takes better care of herself physically. She tries to celebrate the gift of each new day as she enjoys the precious gift of her grandchildren.

The recovery process for victims of sexual abuse is slow. These women have built walls of protection around their hearts and have difficulty admitting to the severity of the abuse. Through years of self-preservation, they have become masters at denying what really happened. So, in order to recover, these women need a safe place where they can learn to trust God and allow Him to teach them how to forgive.

I believe that only God can give women the grace and strength to recover from such deep wounds. Only He can take their shame and transform them into His new creations.

Abuse Setups

Sexual abuse usually unfolds in four stages. The same pattern doesn't hold true in every abuse situation, but it helps to look at the typical sequence. In the first stage, the perpetrator seeks to gain trust and intimacy. This setup may happen well before the first incidence of abuse. Nevertheless, the perpetrator forms a special relationship with the child that includes rewards. To an attention-starved child, this relationship is like a cool drink of water on a parched throat.

Laura began taking swimming lessons when she was eight. She came from a family where both of her parents were emotionally distant, so it felt good when the coach bragged that she was his star pupil. He often held her around the waist in the water as he moved her arms in the motion of a new swimming stroke. When she finished swimming, he would wrap a towel around her and hug her.

Physical contact is a part of stage two, and the contact seems to be appropriate. Still, a special bond forms for the child as the intimacy of the relationship increases. The desire for this affection on the child's part is not sexual, but is a normal God-given need.

When Laura reached puberty, the coach began to make comments about her lovely long legs and developing breasts. Laura felt uncomfortable and weird, but her confusion was pushed aside by the enjoyment of someone thinking she was special. It wasn't long before the coach began to put his hand into her swimsuit during private lessons to fondle her.

The third stage involves the actual abuse.

Finally, the fourth stage of abuse is similar to the first in that the abuser seeks to maintain secrecy and intimacy. So, true to this pattern, the coach warned Laura that if she ever told anyone about their special relationship, she would never be able to compete again. He also often gave her privileges of candy and spending money to use at swim meets.

Sexual abuse brings up a host of different emotions. Many clients have explained that—to their dismay—they experienced physical pleasure. Feeling terror and pleasure at the same time makes for an especially intense confusion, which often causes the victim to feel shame and self-blame. God created our bodies to enjoy sexual arousal. Arousal is normal. The abuse of these feelings makes victims feel that their own body betrayed them.

Wounded Hearts

Picture yourself out gardening one afternoon. As you dig in the soil, getting it ready to plant beautiful flowers, you suddenly feel a sharp pain in your index finger. You brush the dirt away and discover a deeply lodged splinter. After heading for the house to wash your hands, you get some antiseptic and a needle and begin the process of trying to pull the splinter out.

No luck. It's in too deep for you to remove it. So, the splinter remains in your finger. Not surprisingly, the area looks swollen, puffy, and red after a few days. Your finger begins to fester around that splinter, and you feel a dull, throbbing pain.

In the same way, each time you are abused during childhood, it's as if the abuser has driven a splinter deep into your heart. The splinter came as an unexpected shock. You never saw it coming and had no way of blocking it. In your helplessness, there was no way to cry out, no one to hear your pain, no way to lash out and express your anger over being hurt so deeply.

Once the splinter of abuse gets lodged, it begins to fester and form an emotional puss wound in your heart. The festering wound needs attention, but you feel incapable of dealing with it. When infections are ignored, they grow into an abscess, which can be frighteningly painful. Consequently, in trying to escape this pain, many fall into addictions that temporarily numb the painful memories of their abusive pasts.

The continued festering of your finger indicates that you should seek medical attention to remove the splinter and heal the infection before it spreads. God has given us this warning system of pain, but we often ignore it and then encounter even graver consequences. For example, when the light comes on the dash of your car indicating you need oil, it doesn't take much effort or money to get the oil changed. But if you ignore that warning light and keep driving your car, eventually you will burn up the engine. Now you have a very large and expensive problem, which could have been avoided by following the warning signal.

We can deal with the hurts of the past now, and it will not be easy. Or we can wait ten to twenty years after we've been through a divorce, picked up an addiction, or reared children who will be stained by our unresolved issues. Remember that we are passing on a family inheritance, and our choices determine what we will give to our children. Waiting to deal with the abuse will only cause more heartache in the future.

Denial

Stacy had been in therapy for about six months to work through depression and bulimia. During one session, in an emotionally flat voice, she said, "This probably isn't important at all, and I've never mentioned this to anyone before, but I thought I should tell you that my grandfather used to fondle me whenever I was in his home." As with all abuse victims, I assured Stacy that what her grandfather did was not her fault.

"You don't understand," she argued. "Some of it had to be my fault. I should have found a way to stop him. So I am just as much at fault as he was."

Again, remember that sexually abused women typically blame themselves. Many turn away from the wound and pretend that they are fine. However, denying the abuse blocks a woman from getting better. We cannot change what we will not acknowledge. Rather, restoration can only begin when the wounds are clearly acknowledged. So, if you have been sexually abused, you need to seek help from a Christian counselor. It takes courage to work through the issues of the past, but cleaning out the past will give you hope of a better future.

CHURCH-RELATED DENIAL
During one session, Ann shared that she had met with her pastor in order to address her sexual abuse and suicidal feelings. In this way, she hoped to get the support of the church as she

struggled through the recovery process. Her pastor patiently listened and then offered a simple prescription.

"You just need to take it to the cross," he said. After she told me about the meeting, she yelled, "And what am I supposed to do with it when I get to the cross?" His pat answer had heaped more guilt and shame on her because she felt if she "could not just let it go," she must not be spiritual enough. It would have been much healthier for the pastor to just admit that he didn't know anything about recovery from sexual abuse, but that he would certainly help her find someone who did.

Sometimes, well-intentioned people tell abused women to look to the future and forget about looking at the past. But that encourages these women to ignore the warning signals that God has placed in their hearts—that something is desperately wrong and needs immediate attention in order to heal.

For some reason, the church tends to steer away from looking at the effects of sin. It seems that we prefer to deny any reality that isn't pretty, and by doing so, we encourage people to "fake it" and act like they're doing well even when their private world is falling apart.

But deeply wounded people cannot just forgive and forget. They can't just erase the videotapes of abuse that linger in their minds. So this advice often makes them feel guilty. In this way, abused women pick up an extra burden of shame by embracing the lie that they must not be spiritually mature enough to forgive and forget. So, another disappointment weighs them down.

The Burden of Shame

Abuse victims rarely come from healthy, stable families. Their family may look good from the outside, but inside the home it is usually dysfunctional in that it lacks relational closeness and acceptance. Every family pattern will vary, but emotional intimacy does not exist in abusive families. This home life sets children up to be hungry and needy for the missing attention and affection.

Sexual abuse is the most damaging and shaming form of all of the abuses, and victims often feel that they are scarred and stained for life. For instance, if they expose the abuse, they fear being misunderstood or judged as abnormal people who are flawed and contaminated by the abuse.

Some people simply feel uncomfortable when they learn of a woman's sexual abuse. They may care, but they often do not know how to respond in a supportive, loving manner. Sadly, the discomfort others express over the abuse encourages the victim to live in denial in order to avoid any awkward situations that could create even more shame.

Abused and shame-filled women fear intimate relationships because to be intimate you must be close, and closeness has caused great pain in the past. Their internal goal becomes to remain safe, but this isolation produces great loneliness. When an abused woman does form a relationship with a man, she generally uses poor judgment in choosing because she does not feel worthy of a truly caring man.

The bottom line is that women who have been sexually abused feel a deep sense of worthlessness and self-hatred. After all, some people cherish objects more than they have been cherished. Therefore, they associate abuse with a lack of personal value. Furthermore, failing to stop the abuse leaves them feeling powerless and helpless to change their current circumstances.

> There are many reasons why sexual memories can be painful. The first is that our sexuality is at the very heart of our identity. Our [sexuality] is deeply wrapped up with who we are and how we view ourselves. Damage to this area is bound to deeply affect our self-esteem.
>
> The second reason is that sex is such a powerful emotion. . . . One of the most terrible facts about child molestation is the awakening of such overwhelming

emotions at such an early age and under such frightening conditions. . . . But perhaps the most important reason these memories are so painful is that sexual feelings can be the most contradictory emotions we humans experience. . . . What [abused women] have undergone can result in their experiencing sex as an incredible combination of desire and dread, pleasure and pain, fascination and fear. This is why unhealed sexual traumas carried into married life often produce a terrible inner conflict of wanting sex but hating it at the same time.[1]

We are all created with the need to be loved for who we are and not for what we do—to be cared for as human beings and not human doings. All children are hungry to be held, hugged, and cherished by a loving parent. But Satan attacks victims with shame by making them feel guilty over their natural longing to be cared for and wanted. The Enemy twists the truth of the way God made us all and shames victims with the lie that the abuse was somehow their own fault because of their neediness. The victim has now begun to hate her legitimate, God-given desires.

Dr. Dan Allender's book on sexual abuse and recovery shows how shame is wrapped into the abuse:

This will help us to understand why shame is such a significant part of sexual abuse. Consider the damage done to the soul when the abuse is fused with the legitimate longings of the heart. The flower of deep longing for love is somehow hideously intertwined with the weed of abuse. Longings are wed to abuse, abuse begets shame and shame is inextricably related to a hatred of one's own hungry soul. Any abuse causes the victim to despise the way he or she's been made: a person wired for deep, satisfying, eternal involvement with others and God.[2]

A Light in the Darkness

"Okay, I realize things need to be worked out and changed in my life, but I'm so afraid and I don't know where to start," some clients say. "I feel like I'm walking around in the dark, searching for a light." I know exactly what that feels like.

When I was nine years old, I spent a week away from home at summer camp for the first time. I struggled with being homesick every day. On Wednesday night, it was camp tradition to take a mile-long hike down a dirt road to sit on "Hangman's Bridge" and listen to ghost stories. I still wonder which brilliant person thought up the idea of taking a hundred petrified nine-year-olds on a long walk in the dark! A canopy of huge trees covered the bridge above. So, on a moonless night, the darkness was thick enough to cut with a knife. You could not see your hand in front of your face.

Terrified doesn't come close to describing the feeling I had as my little heart pounded in my chest! One of the rules was that no camper was allowed to use a flashlight. Only a few counselors carried them. Fortunately, my cabin counselor was one of the chosen few with a priceless light to illuminate the dark night and the dirt road.

My poor counselor—I'm surprised that she could walk because in my fear, I tried hard to become her Siamese twin. I became attached at her hip and held on to her for dear life. I knew that as long as I stayed close to her I could see, and nothing could get me. She was kind and understanding about my fear. She even allowed me to sit close beside her during the ghost stories, and I felt safe while she kept her arm around me.

Whenever I reminisce about those days, I remember Psalm 119:105: "Your word is a lamp to my feet and a light for my path." Psalm 18:28 also comes to mind: "You, O LORD, keep my lamp burning; my God turns my darkness into light."

There are many times in life when we feel like a frightened child trying to walk in the dark on an unknown pathway. When I'm afraid, I want to sit down and not even try to move forward.

But in the same way that it comforted me to know that my human counselor had a flashlight and knew where she was going, we can have confidence and peace knowing that God views the entire pathway ahead of us.

He has been there before. As a matter of fact, He's the creator of the path, so He knows the complete map of what's ahead. When we feel lost and afraid, we can turn to God's Word and find a light that pierces through the darkest night to help us find direction and safety.

A Root of Bitterness on the Path of Forgiveness

Because it's spring, I've been in the mood to plant. When I finished the outdoor plants, I decided I should re-pot the indoor plants. I bought larger containers and new potting soil, and I started dragging plants outside to avoid a really dirty mess. As I took the first plant out of its old container, I was shocked that no dirt crumbled out. All I could see was a large mass of roots. The plant had been in the same container for so long that it had used up most of the dirt and become root bound. Everywhere I looked, I found a massive, tangled root system.

When we choose not to forgive, the roots of bitterness in our heart are very much like that plant. These roots begin to take over everything in sight. Pretty soon, those roaming roots touch every area of our life. The more embedded the roots of bitterness become, the more difficult they are to pull out.

There are so many marriage relationships, friendships, and parent-to-child relationships that have been damaged by anger over something that happened many years ago. Those bitterly unresolved issues bleed into every relationship. Hebrews 12:15 teaches that a bitter root grows up to cause trouble and defile many.

"I can never forgive because that lets my abuser off the hook," you may say. "If I forget what he did, he'll go unpunished!"

Consider this: your lack of forgiveness does not necessarily damage your abuser. Yet, it can ruin your life. The abuser may have no idea that you are suffering with anger and unforgiveness.

To harbor bitter unforgiveness would be like addressing your abuser and saying, "I am furious with you for what you've done. Here, take that!" In this case, "that" means watching as you repeatedly bang your head against a concrete wall. You're the one getting the headache, and the abuser is not suffering one bit.

Philip Yancey explains this need for forgiveness well: "If we do not transcend nature, we remain bound to the people we cannot forgive, held in their vise grip. This principle applies even when one party is wholly innocent and the other wholly to blame, for the innocent party will bear the wound until he or she can find a way to release it—and forgiveness is the only way."[3]

I fully believe that without the help of the Holy Spirit, we are not capable of forgiveness. On my own, I want revenge, not forgiveness! I've been known to play a mental movie over and over again of how I will pay back a person who has hurt or humiliated me. It is only when I come to understand that I do not deserve God's gift of forgiveness in Christ that I can begin to get a picture of true forgiveness.

If I got what I deserve, I would spend eternity in hell. I owed a debt for my sin that I could not possibly pay. Praise God that He paid the debt He did not owe when He died for my sin! Now, I can view the example of forgiveness set for me by Christ. In offering forgiveness to those who have harmed me, I give to others what I have so lavishly received from God.

Romans 5:8 states, "God demonstrates his own love for us in this: While we were still sinners, Christ died for us." I love this verse! It says that God didn't wait until I could be good enough, pray hard enough, or otherwise clean up my act enough before He would forgive me. Instead, He comes to us with His abundant grace in all of our sin and ashes and offers us the gift of salvation and hope. In our darkest moment, He comes in to lift us up, clean us up, and adopt us into His family.

But before you can forgive others, you must forgive yourself. In college, I used to verbally and emotionally castigate myself whenever I did anything wrong. When I sinned, I figured I had to pay penance for it to make certain that I really suffered and was miserable for my wrongdoing. One day, a friend asked me if I believed in God's grace and forgiveness.

"Well, of course I do," I replied.

"So, do you believe that God has forgiven you?" she continued.

"Well, sure I believe that God has forgiven me," I answered.

"That's pretty interesting," she said, "because your standards are higher than God's. You won't forgive yourself."

I think my jaw hit the floor as I realized she was right. I was setting my standard of forgiveness on a higher level than God's. Do you believe that God forgives you? Can you forgive yourself? If you cannot forgive yourself, remember that forgiveness is a process. Somehow we think it's an instant thing, and that if we can't forgive and forget, then we're obviously not spiritually mature.

If we look at the life of Christ—and He's the one who purchased our redemption and gave us forgiveness—we see that the forgiveness He gave did not happen overnight. Genesis 3:15 predicts the coming of a Savior after Adam and Eve sinned. But it took 4,000 years for Christ to step into human flesh. His earthly ministry took thirty-three years, and His death and resurrection took three days. Taking the time you need to forgive is not a sign of spiritual weakness, but you do need to get started.

What if I told you that by simply walking through a doorway you could immediately lose ten pounds? Most women would knock each other down in a stampede trying to get through that doorway! You would run faster for that than if I yelled "Fire!" But did you know that you could emotionally and spiritually lose the weight of a burdened heart if you would be willing to walk toward, and eventually through, the doorway of forgiveness?

As the years go by, it becomes increasingly difficult to drag around the ball and chain of a bitter spirit. God wants to set you free by teaching you to forgive. It won't necessarily be an instantaneous experience. You may have to start today by praying, "Dear God, please make me *willing* to forgive." But that is the first step toward letting go of the past and walking in the present.

I once read an anonymous quote that said, "Forgiveness is a gift I give myself." At first, I thought it wasn't a very "spiritual" idea. Then, I began to realize that when we forgive others, we set ourselves free from the bondage of bitterness.

> Forgiveness is difficult. The first and often the only person to be healed by forgiveness is the person who does the forgiving. . . When we genuinely forgive, we set a prisoner free and then discover that the prisoner we set free was us.[4]

I learned a lot about the power of forgiveness from my client Ann—the woman who was abused by seven men. After about three years in counseling, she attended a family Christmas gathering. That afternoon, she found her older brother—the one who had done the greatest amount of abuse—alone in one of the rooms. She went into that room and said, "I don't need for you to respond, but I want you to know that because I have learned how much Christ has forgiven me, I forgive you for the things you have done to me." She then turned and left the room.

When she reported this to me the next week, I could only sit and cry over the power of God's grace to change lives. What a testimony to her unsaved brother.

God Uses Our Past

Whatever your circumstances, recovery involves realizing that *you cannot get a new past.* You can move to a new state where no one knows you, start a new job, or marry another person, but the hurt will follow you. You can lie about it, change the story, say it doesn't really matter and didn't affect you, but you cannot make it go away until you face it head on. It doesn't matter how hard you try to pretend that nothing really happened, that it wasn't really that bad, or that life now is going well.

Who you are today is a combination of all the events that have occurred in your past. You have been shaped by the events of your past, and denying the negative events won't make them go away. Remember that God is in the business of taking the shameful parts of the past and turning them into something valuable that He can use in the lives of others. But God can only transform your ashes into something beautiful when you admit you have lots of ash and begin turning it over to Him.

Christian counselors can help you work toward wholeness, and support groups can offer you hope and encouragement. Ann still has her ups and downs, but by seeking help in her recovery process, she discovered the truth—that the abuse was not her fault.

You too can learn to embrace and accept yourself as the precious woman God intended. Seek, and you will find forgiveness through the matchless healing power of the Lord Jesus Christ. Give God your wounded heart—His truth will set you free!

seven

A /HAMEFUL "CHOICE": DEALING WITH THE /HAME OF ABORTION

A voice is heard in Ramah,
mourning and great weeping,
Rachel weeping for her children and
refusing to be comforted,
because her children are no more.
JEREMIAH 31:15

entered the lobby of the counseling center and introduced myself to Cara, a neatly dressed, attractive woman in her early forties. During our first counseling session, she told me that she had been struggling with depression for several years. However, it seemed to be getting worse lately. In fact, she claimed it had kept her from participating in her normal daily activities. Cara had two children in their early teens and was worried about how her depression was affecting them.

She cried throughout that first session as she explained the internal darkness she was experiencing as well as the frustration of being overweight. Her eating had gotten out of control.

During our next session, Cara shared that her marriage had been very difficult from the start.

As I got to know her, I realized that she made a classic example of generational sin. Her father was an alcoholic infamous for his drunken rages. So as a child, Cara remembers her mother waking her up and taking her away from the house in order to protect her from those domestic storms. Cara, in turn, later married a man who was similar to her father in that he did not know how to communicate with her or the children. He always seemed emotionally absent—even without the distraction of alcohol.

By the end of our fifth session, Cara handed me a letter. I asked if she would like to read it to me, and her face looked stricken with panic. Tears brimmed in her eyes, and her voice trembled as she stood in the doorway of my office and said, "If you read this and don't want me to come back again, I will understand." She seemed heavy with guilt and grief as she left that session.

As I read the letter later that evening, I began to get a much better understanding of the pain in Cara's life. Ten years before coming to counseling, she had become pregnant with a third child and had an abortion.

Here's the story in her own words: "When I went to the doctor, it never entered my mind that I was pregnant with our third child. The other children were only one and four. I was surprised when the doctor told me the test results that day.

"I don't think I 'connected' at the time with the fact that I was carrying a child. I didn't even make the suggested appointment to get the blood work done or to have the vitamin prescription filled. It was as if I knew subconsciously that I couldn't have the baby without even thinking about it.

"The doctor said that he would tell my husband for me if I wished. I don't remember why he would have said that except that I must have told him that I couldn't tell my husband myself. I declined the offer. I don't remember telling my husband, but I know I did. The pregnancy never seemed real to me.

"My marriage had never been good. My two children were a

handful because my husband never helped care for them. We were never a family. I had just gone back to work, and our finances were finally livable. When I tried to talk to my husband about the baby, he told me that he didn't know if he would stick around to raise the two children we had, but he was fairly certain he would not stay with a third child.

"I believed him. It was not up for discussion. I remember thinking, 'What do I have to do to keep this family together?' I felt like keeping the family together was all up to me, as was most everything else that involved our children.

"In addition to my husband, I also told my parents and my sister. I think that along with telling them I was pregnant, I also told them that we would be getting an abortion. I explained to them what I had been told, that it was just another form of birth control. It sounded like a good reason, and I tried to rationalize to myself that it was valid. If I didn't really think about it then I might buy into it.

"My parents had to know because I needed Mother to stay with the kids while my husband took me for the procedure. My father said all along that we were doing the right thing because we couldn't afford another baby.

"A few days after making the appointment for the abortion, I remember hugging my husband and crying. I told him I wished that somehow we could keep the baby. I wanted his comfort during this horribly difficult time. He never gave me the slightest indication that we could consider not having the abortion. Rather, he would reaffirm 'our' decision and say that we had to go through with it.

"I told him I wished he wanted the baby too, so that we could keep it. But I never thought about not going along with his wishes on this matter. I can't even connect with the thought of hugging him now. It's been too many years, and we are way too emotionally distant. I know that I still cannot look to him for comfort.

"The day came for him to drive me to the abortion [clinic]. My mother came over to keep the children for me, and I called in sick to work. I felt nauseated and sobbed the whole way to the clinic. The staff tried to reassure me by saying, 'This is a legal procedure. Another child would complicate your life. This is the best decision for you.' I wanted to scream out, 'No it's not the best decision! I don't want to be here!'

"Instead, I tried to calm down by telling myself it would all be over soon. They gave me a shot of something that would relax me, and I remember my first and immediate response was that I didn't want anything that would 'hurt the baby.'

"Later, in the recovery area, I pulled the brown wool blanket they gave me over my head and wished I could escape and disappear from the world. In the following weeks, I would sort of wake up and wander into the nursery area where my one-year-old daughter was sleeping. I had felt the need to 'feed the baby.' Every other time I had been pregnant the result was a baby to feed.

"Then, I would wake up enough to realize there was no baby. I would go back to bed and cry myself to sleep. That was a horrible feeling. Twenty years later, I still can't believe I went through an abortion with as strong a maternal instinct as I have.

"To this day, I cannot go to the dentist without having horrible flashbacks of the abortion. The sound of the drill is so much like the sound of the equipment that took my baby out of my body. I was prepared for the physical pain after the abortion, but I had no way of knowing how excruciating the emotional pain of the abortion would be."

Knowing the Truth

The baby growing inside the mother's body isn't just a "fetus" or "product of conception" or "tissue" or even a generic "baby," but a one-of-a-kind, intentionally designed, and uniquely created human being. The medical term "fetus" is Latin for "little one," and we should consider this when we use the term without a thought of what it actually denotes.

Though very tiny, this "little one" is growing and developing in a marvelous way.[1] Dr. Paul Rockwell of Troy, New York, witnessed firsthand one of God's smallest creations when he laid eyes on an eight-week-old fetus, the product of a ruptured tubal pregnancy.

> I was handed what appeared to be the smallest human being ever seen. The embryo sac was still intact and transparent. Within the sac was a tiny (one third inch) human male swimming extremely vigorously in the amniotic fluid, while attached to the wall by the umbilical cord. This tiny human was perfectly developed with long tapering fingers, feet and toes. It was almost transparent as regards to the skin, and the delicate arteries and veins were prominent to the ends of the fingers. The baby was extremely alive.[2]

Post Abortion Syndrome

Most women do not choose abortion without an emotional struggle, and a woman who aborts often feels desperate for one reason or another. She may know that the father is unsupportive. She may also realize how much a child will radically alter her future. Others abort because they cannot face the shame of an out-of-wedlock pregnancy. Some don't want to disappoint their parents by admitting the promiscuity.

To make matters worse, after undergoing an abortion, some suffer a form of Post Traumatic Stress Disorder known as Post Abortion Syndrome (PAS). Even long after the incident, a woman may develop emotional or physical reactions to the abortion. Symptoms may not appear together, and most women will not suffer from all of them.

I diagnosed Cara with PAS because she had nightmares about being pregnant and having dead babies. She also struggled with unresolved guilt and anguish—especially when she looked at her two children and thought that she could have aborted them. She couldn't forgive herself and feared that anyone who found out about the abortion would reject her.

Cara truly believed the lie that her punishment for life was to carry the unhealed burden of the abortion. Many women also link other painful events that occur later in life as punishment for what they did that fateful day. In Cara's case, she used food to comfort herself in the midst of this shame and then gained unwanted weight, which made her feel even worse.

A woman feels guilt when she internalizes her decision to kill an unborn child. Before the abortion, she may have believed it was only a "blob" of tissue being removed from her body. But as time goes on, she may experience a change of heart when she sees a sonogram or goes through a full-term pregnancy and learns that a baby's heartbeat begins eighteen days after conception.

Not surprisingly, depression is another PAS symptom, which can lead to suicidal thoughts. Women experiencing PAS may consider suicide as one way to ease the pain or to commit the ultimate punishment. Depression often makes them feel worthlessness and hopelessness. It involves constant sadness and, in some cases, bouts of uncontrollable crying.

Depression also can cause insomnia and eating problems. For instance, some women have no appetite when they are depressed, and other women will overeat to comfort themselves. A depressed woman may lose interest in participating in her daily activities. She may also isolate herself because she feels unable to communicate—especially with a boyfriend or husband if they were involved in the abortion.

Frequently, anxiety and irritability flank depression. Anxiety and irritability make the woman feel agitated and unable to concentrate or remember. She may suffer from stress-related nausea and headaches and, at times, feel inexplicably restless.

Despite these PAS symptoms, affected women often go into denial; they shut down emotionally to make certain that they are never vulnerable enough to be hurt again. But when they cut off their ability to feel the pain of the abortion, they also shut down their ability to feel any other emotions. In this way, denial can prevent women from enjoying close relationships with others and with God. After all, seeking intimacy with others and with God requires a vulnerability that she is afraid to allow.

Therefore, it didn't surprise me when Cara mentioned that she's noticed certain triggers that cause flashbacks of the abortion. For her, the sound of the dentist's drill was a trigger. Others suffering from PAS cannot handle the sound of a vacuum because these are similar to sounds they heard during the abortion. Still others may get painful flashbacks when they see a newborn baby, undergo an annual gynecological exam, or drive past a building that looks like the clinic where her abortion was performed.

Furthermore, PAS women typically become more symptomatic around the yearly anniversary of the abortion or at the time of the unmet due date. Those triggers may give them nightmares of crying babies or aborted babies.

Untreated PAS victims are vulnerable to addictions—from drugs and alcohol to eating disorders—because the addiction can temporarily dull the emotional pain and guilt surrounding the abortion. Substance abuse is a common form of self-medicating depression and anxiety, but it only leads to more problems. What begins as a way to numb depression ends up increasing it since drugs and alcohol are depressants.

Dealing with Anger

Anger turned inward becomes depression. Therefore, some suffering from PAS and its related depression may need to deal with their anger. Ignoring anger will never resolve it. And anger from the past can act as a roadblock to healing by festering and causing more bitterness.

To move forward in the healing process, you may need to deal with your anger toward the father of the child you aborted, particularly if he refused to offer you emotional and financial support, or if he took you to the abortion clinic. You may feel anger toward the workers at the clinic who withheld the truth about the procedure. Like so many other women, you may also feel angry with yourself for being in a sexual situation in the first place, and for being afraid to have the baby. Some even feel angry with God for allowing the pregnancy to occur.

Once you are in touch with your anger, it's important that you learn how best to express it. When you are unable to express your anger, you become a "stuffer." For instance, assume that you are only set up to hold five hundred dollars' worth of anger in your emotional savings account. However, as you continue to stuff your anger, you collect two thousand dollars' worth of anger.

When that happens, when you stuff so much anger beyond what you're set up to hold, you change and become a "spewer." If someone angers you, and that person's action deserves about a dollar's worth of anger in response, you will spew out fifty dollars' worth of anger or more in his or her direction.

Spewers seem unable to control their emotional responses, and they're not even sure why. People who receive an "anger spew" wonder what in the world they did wrong, and what is the matter with the person spewing. What could cause such an explosive response? Finally, when anger is expressed as rage—a more intense and sustained form of spewing—it goes beyond ruffling another's feathers. It can be out of control, damaging, and violent.

"I decided while going through a recovery Bible study that there was no way I could ever be angry enough with my husband to counterbalance out the abortion," Cara explained during a session in which we discussed anger. "For years I thought, 'Let's see, just how much anger would I have to put on the scale to equal the situation of aborting the baby?' I realized that as God had forgiven me, so I needed to forgive my husband even if he never asked for forgiveness. How he deals with the abortion is between him and God. I had to let go of the anger."

But letting go of anger is tough when you can't manage to acknowledge it. To begin dealing honestly with your anger, ask for God's help. He will guide you through it one step at a time. If you have been through an abortion, I encourage you to call your local pregnancy crisis center to sign up for a recovery Bible study. Leaders there can offer specific help for reconciling all of your emotions regarding the abortion.

You may even decide that you need to have time in individual therapy with a Christian counselor, especially if you are struggling with addiction, anxiety, or depression. When I counsel angry women, I encourage them to write letters that will never be mailed. The first sentence begins, "I am angry because. . . ." From there, try expressing all your feelings of rejection, rage, betrayal, and hurt.

Grieving the Loss

After an abortion, a woman may initially experience relief. She may feel liberated from facing the consequences of her pregnancy. Sadly, however, the very act that seemed to provide relief soon begins to create its own form of misery. One of my clients shared that she felt afraid to get in touch with her grief.

"I know that if I had a child that died after being born, I would be heartbroken. I realize now that this is the same loss for me. But if I start to feel the sadness of the abortion, I am scared that it is such a huge ocean of pain that I will fall into it and drown."

But God designed mourning as a way for us to release our pain and begin to heal. When we grieve for someone, it is an expression of love for the other person. Grieving is a sign of love for the baby you lost.

During biblical times, you clearly knew when someone was grieving. They tore their clothes and rubbed ashes on their faces. Many of them sat in the middle of the street and wailed! Even as recently as the Civil War, widows wore black clothes for a year to show that they were grieving the loss of their husband.

Unfortunately, our society pressures people to be tough like a "John Wayne" and get over pain quickly. But God who designed us in His own image did not create us that way. Grief is not an emotion that we get over, it is one that we must walk through and experience. Don't worry if it takes time. You may have stored these painful emotions for years, but letting out the tears is cleansing.

Isaiah 60:20 states, "The LORD will be your everlasting light, and your days of sorrow will end." Hold tightly to God, and find comfort in knowing that grief can cleanse and heal your wounded heart. Soon the grief will pass, and Psalm 126:5 says you will find joy!

Consequences

"I just wish I could go back to the time when I was seventeen," wept Samantha, a forty-something client of mine. "I could go to sleep at night back then with a clear conscience because I had not made any major mistakes in life. Now I lie in bed at night and can't go to sleep for all the guilt that floods into my mind. Each night is a recital of all my failures, starting out with the sexually promiscuous relationship with my boyfriend.

"Then I get to the abortion, and I hate myself for killing my first and only child. I believed that abortion was a 'quick fix,' a hidden solution to a private problem and that no one would ever have to know about it. I have never been able to have children since then, and I know the infertility is God's way of punishing me."

"The infertility is not God's way of punishing you," I explained. "As long as Satan can keep you believing that lie, then you remain too angry with God to seek a healing relationship with Him. The truth is that all of the punishment for our sins was placed on Christ as He died on the cross.

"You've made it clear that you are very sorry and repentant for the abortion," I added. "Discipline only comes when we refuse to be repentant for our sin. In that case, Hebrews 12:7-11 says that God disciplines us as a loving parent would. His discipline is to bring us back into an obedient relationship with Him. Your infertility may well be a consequence of the abortion, but it is not a punishment."

With a look of confusion, Samantha admitted that she didn't understand the difference between a punishment and a consequence.

"Try this," I responded. "If you forget to put a gallon of ice cream back in the freezer before you go to bed at night, the next morning the ice cream will be melted and ruined. That is a consequence of leaving out the ice cream. It isn't a punishment for your forgetfulness, but a consequence of a warm kitchen counter."

"I think I am starting to understand," Samantha replied. "What you're trying to tell me is that God did not plan out my infertility as a punishment for my abortion. The infertility occurred due to the consequence of damage to my reproductive organs during the abortion. If I had chosen to keep the child, the consequences would be entirely different."

"Now you're starting to see the truth," I confirmed. "Another truth I want to assure you of is that God still loves you just the way He did when you were seventeen—before you think you started making big mistakes. His love for you doesn't change! He grieves over our sin because He hates for us to suffer from our disobedience, and He knows that sin separates us from an intimate relationship with Him. But He is always waiting to welcome us back into the sweet fellowship of relationship with Him. He is the perfect parent, and loves us no matter what we've done."

Recovery and Support

Cara and Samantha both went through a recovery Bible study. Through it, they learned that other people could know about the abortion and still be loving toward them. Samantha said that the other women in the group became "Jesus with skin on." "They showed me the love of Christ by listening to me with unconditional acceptance, and one woman even held my hand as I cried and shared my story. That was so important in helping me realize that God still loved me and forgave me."

There is also great freedom in a group of women who have gone through the same experience because you realize that others have the same thoughts and emotions you are dealing with. You are no longer the "only one" who has gone through this.

"Toward the end of the study, we were given the assignment to identify our baby," Cara recalls. "The most important thing I learned was when God revealed to me that I have a son in heaven. I saw for the first time that God loves my son and me even more than I could possibly imagine. I knew that I could release the burden to God where it belonged. I knew that my family would be complete in heaven one day. I felt that God gave me permission to 'let go' and finally receive His forgiveness."

During the past ten years, Cara has led many Bible studies for women who have had abortions, and she has given her testimony publicly. She told me recently that she would have never chosen to lead these Bible studies, but she feels that God clearly called her into this ministry to women who are hurting just as she once was.

"I'm completely healed and at peace with God's love and forgiveness of me, though I will always deeply regret taking the life of my son," she shared.

When my clients say that they cannot forgive themselves for what they have done, I know that they have not yet accepted God's forgiveness. If you've had an abortion, you need to know that you are not alone in this healing process, and that you need not continue carrying a load of guilt and shame.

God is able to heal even the most damaged heart brought before Him. He is the real answer to our painful problems, and He can work in ways we simply don't think are possible. God can, and will, give a woman peace and freedom from a past abortion.

Cara's story of healing and ministry to others is not unusual. Miraculous? Yes. Amazing? Yes. But, her experience is not unusual. Her life today is a living portrait of God's grace. He has taken her most painful mistake and reshaped it in a way that now blesses the lives of other women who have made the same painful choice.

God is the God of healing and grace in reshaping our deepest shame and using it for His glory. In the same way that God gave Cara "beauty for ashes," He is waiting to do the same for you.

eight

MY BODY, MY ENEMY: EXAMINING BODY IMAGE AND EATING DISORDERS

Create in me a pure heart, O God,
and renew a steadfast spirit within me.
Do not cast me from your presence
or take your Holy Spirit from me.
Restore to me the joy of your salvation.
PSALM 51:10-12

Turn on the television, glance at a billboard, read any newspaper or magazine and you will see tall, extremely thin young women using sex and the image of perfection to sell everything from cars and cola to toothpaste. However, if you check out those shopping at the mall, worshiping at church, or gathering their children from school, you'll see a society full of overweight women. And these women typically struggle with their appearance every morning when they look into the mirror.

Women who struggle with eating disorders are trapped in the cycle of addiction. Most have typically grown up in dysfunctional families but tend to deny that there were any problems. Their parents may have used perfectionistic standards or manipulated them through shame and guilt in order to control their behaviors.

> These children learn to cope by developing "unhealthy patterns," [which] often include an intense need for control and an enmeshment with the family; children lose their identity, fear acknowledging or expressing feelings and have a heightened sense of worthlessness. Children in this type of family develop a love hunger because their parents are not showing them the love and affection they need to mature to healthy, happy adults.[1]

> Control is also a big issue for a child growing up in an unhealthy family. In a dysfunctional family with an alcoholic parent or where there are sexual, physical or emotional abuses, the child grows up learning to be scared. In defense, they take control of their lives to protect themselves from pain.
>
> As the child grows older, there are only a few battlegrounds where they can practice their control. Money is one of them. It's not unusual for a binge eater to become a binge spender or a compulsive gambler. Ironically, most compulsive eaters are over disciplined. They tell themselves, "If I can just have more willpower I could beat this food issue. I could make that diet work with a little more willpower." Yet, willpower is not the answer. Believing you can solve the problem with just a little more self-control often leads to binge eating each time this faulty approach fails.[2]

Secrets do not have to be extraordinary to be powerful, and keeping the secret of an eating disorder is part of the addiction pattern. Compulsive overeaters are not able to hide their addiction because they are overweight and often obese. But other eating-related addictions like bulimia and anorexia may be more easily concealed.

For instance, bulimics usually weigh within ten to fifteen pounds of their ideal body weight, and they purge privately. Anorexic behavior can be cleverly hidden, too. However, it will eventually become noticeable when the woman can't bring herself to eat with others, and when her body weight drops so far below her ideal that the baggiest clothes can't hide her gauntness.

Eating disorders involve food, but the main issue for women with eating disorders is the emotional pain they are trying to avoid. Focusing on the food helps them ignore the unresolved hurts in their hearts. As with other addictions, eating disorders always begin with pain. The pain may trace back to dysfunctional dynamics in the family of origin, or it may be caused by a trauma, or it may relate to poor self-worth.

As pain increases, the suffering person finds an anesthesia to avoid dealing with the aching emotions. The compulsive overeater binges on large amounts of food without purging, so her weight gain is evident to others. The bulimic binges on large amounts of food and then purges to avoid gaining weight. The anorectic avoids food, even though her thoughts are always about food and how to control her eating. Yet, all three have this in common: they seek to control their food in various ways as an attempt to control their disturbing, unidentified emotions.

Food-related rituals represent another way for this type of addict to get some sense of control. The rituals may seem strange to others, but these women feel comforted by the familiar patterns they set up. Rituals may involve the time and place food is purchased and eaten to the types and amounts of food that are consumed. I have counseled bulimics who ritualistically hide stashes of food in order to eat in secret or anorectics who only eat apples and strawberries.

As with all addictions, there is a fix or a high associated with the "drug of choice." For a few moments after abusing food, both the compulsive overeater and the bulimic feel a sense of relief from anxiety. The anorectic, on the other hand, feels the power of control when she successfully starves herself all day. But soon, all three come down from the high and are left with tremendous shame, guilt, and self-loathing, which jumpstarts another cycle.

Case Studies

THE COMPULSIVE OVEREATER

Maria has struggled with being overweight since childhood. In her family of origin, food was the ultimate source of comfort. When she felt sad after a spat with a friend at her elementary school, she cured her blues with a cold glass of milk and her mother's chocolate chip cookies—as much as she could eat. Eating became Maria's way to calm down after a test or feel some solace when she was tired, lonely, or hurt.

But Maria's family, which is full of compulsive overeaters, also uses food to celebrate happiness. No wonder food got tied up into all of Maria's emotions! Consequently, as an adult, she continued using food as a way to alter her mood.

By her mid-thirties, Maria worried that even her closest friends were ashamed of being seen with her in public. She dreaded going to restaurants because she felt people saw her obese body and then disapprovingly watched how much food she would eat. She felt embarrassed when she dropped a bite of food because it would fall on her chest—not on the napkin in her lap—and it had to be cleaned off.

Criticizing herself for being fat made her feel hurt emotionally, which drove her to seek out the comfort of her old friend food again. It seemed like a never-ending cycle of addiction. While overeating offered temporary relief, she gained weight and felt miserable in the long run.

THE BULIMIC

Mindy grew up with a father who was a raging alcoholic. Her

father would come in drunk and yell at her if anything was out of place in her bedroom. She interpreted herself as "bad" and felt that if she could only be good, her father would not be so angry all the time. That explains how Mindy moved into the role of a perfectionistic people pleaser. She pushed all of the anger she felt toward her father deep inside and focused instead on keeping peace in her home.

As an adult, Mindy has struggled with bulimia for seventeen years. She was about ten pounds over her desired weight in college, but wasn't too concerned. Then, during spring break one year, she and a sorority sister shared a pizza together. After they finished eating, the other girl said, "I have to get rid of this," and walked toward the bathroom.

"What are you doing?" Mindy asked. That night Mindy learned how to purge her food by vomiting. It seemed to be the perfect answer for how to eat all she wanted and not gain weight. But what started out in college as a weekly purge has over the years become an addiction, which takes place several times a day. At times she seems to be bulimarectic as she swings between the binge and purge cycle of a bulimic and the starvation associated with anorectics. Often, Mindy entertains suicidal thoughts, but she resists acting on them because she can't bear to hurt her children like that.

In exploring her issue, Mindy told me that all her time alone seems to set her up for a binge. Her husband works long hours and is very emotionally distant. So, she feels a deep loneliness. Evenings tend to be her most difficult time. She eventually recognized that she binges at night to fill her emotional emptiness, however ineffectively.

Getting weekly individual therapy has helped Mindy see how she avoids her own emotions. Consequently, her work in counseling involves getting in touch with her emotions and learning new ways to nurture herself that do not involve food.

"How do you respond when your five-year-old daughter is upset?" I once asked.

"I try to comfort her and find out what the problem is," Mindy replied.

"Well, I have another suggestion," I responded. "The next time she's sad, why don't you force her to eat a dozen doughnuts. Then take her to the bathroom, shove your fingers down her throat, and force her to vomit. I'm sure she will feel much better after that."

"You must be sick," Mindy said, indignant. "I would never do that to my daughter!"

"I just thought if it was good enough for you, it must be good enough for her," I explained.

"I think I understand what you are saying," Mindy said while staring at the floor and watching the tears fall onto her shoes. "I would never do that to my own daughter because I love her. I guess if I learned to love myself, I wouldn't do it to me either."

The Anorectic

Six months ago, Christy's boyfriend broke up with her. He told her that because she had gained ten pounds, he no longer felt attracted to her. At age twenty-two, Christy felt devastated and wondered if any other man would ever care for her. Getting her boyfriend back was out of her control, but she soon found an area that she could control in the midst of her grief—she could control her weight.

Christy's thinking became so distorted that she felt proud of herself if she ate less than 500 calories a day. In this way, by eating celery and carrots only, she dropped from 130 pounds to 95 pounds. Her quick and extreme weight loss worried her family and friends, but whenever they shared their concern, she would tell herself that they were merely jealous of her new figure. However, when she looked at herself in the mirror, she saw a fat body and would vow to lose more weight.

Eventually, she began suffering from dizzy spells and a heart flutter. After she fainted at work, her parents brought her to a hospital eating-disorder unit in the hopes of sparing her life. They considered the hospital the best recovery environment. Indeed, Christy got the support she needed both from the staff and the other women in the program. Her recovery will take some time, but she is now in a safe place where she can no longer continue to starve herself.

What Is an Eating Disorder?

All eating disorders, whether they involve compulsive overeating, bingeing and purging, abusing laxatives, or self-starvation are based on shameful thoughts of unworthiness. Such thoughts and feelings lead these women into self-destructive patterns of behavior.

Those ignorant about eating disorders often think that these women should be able to just "get over it." But eating disorders can be serious addictions that involve extensive treatment. The root issues are often thorny and, if left undiagnosed and untreated, can destroy the women's health to the point of death.

Suzanne Schlosberg explains it this way:

> The results of starvation and over exercising can be severe, including loss of your menstrual period, irreversible bone loss, even a fatal heart attack.[3]

Bulimia can lead to vomiting blood due to either inflammation of the esophagus or stress on the stomach lining. Bulimics often destroy the enamel on their teeth with all the undue stomach acid, and some have scarred their knuckles on their teeth by pushing their fingers down their throats to induce the vomiting.

Women struggling with eating disorders are desperate to gain some control over food because the rest of their life is so out of control. However, many who suffer miss the point that, in reality, their obsession with food and calories controls them.

Perfectionism is a key issue for women with eating disorders. They set unrealistically high goals and think that if they can achieve these goals, they will somehow be able to feel good about themselves. But any drive toward perfection is doomed from the start. Why? God never designed us to be perfect, and perfectionism sets up a person for that discouraging all-or-nothing, black-or-white thinking.

When you expect yourself to be a ten on a scale of one to ten, you've set yourself up for unrealistic standards and this leads to feeling like a failure. Feeling like a failure is painful, and that pain starts the cycle of addiction as the woman seeks to numb her pain again.

For this reason, it's not uncommon for women who have been sexually abused or had an abortion to struggle with compulsive overeating. After all, many women believe that by gaining a substantial amount of weight they will make themselves less attractive to men. The weight is a way to shield her from the possibility of being pursued as a sexual partner. Abstinence ensures that she will not become pregnant again. The food also comforts her emotionally and anesthetizes the pain of the abuse or abortion.

Anorexia is another way women make themselves sexually unattractive. For instance, underweight women lose their breast and hip curves as well as their menstrual cycle, which prevents pregnancy. Becoming physically unattractive supports the anorectic's distorted idea that she is really unworthy of anyone's attention. The shame she feels over abuse or abortion drives her into this self-destructive behavior and can keep her there.

The Road to Recovery

If you grew up in a dysfunctional family, it may be difficult to find a truthful view of God. For instance, many women from dysfunctional families see Him as a harsh, perfectionistic judge who blames them for their mistakes. Therefore, it is difficult for a compulsive overeater, bulimic, or anorectic to understand that God loves her right where she is, no matter what she has done, no matter how she feels.

When the truth of God's unconditional love is finally understood, there is great freedom for these women. Those who experience an intimate relationship with Him appreciate this relationship as one of safety. They learn that He will never reject them, but will give them the strength to live a healthier life.

In the *Message*, Romans 12:1-3 says:

> So here's what I want you to do, God helping you: Take your everyday, ordinary life—your sleeping, eating, going-to-work, and walking-around life—and place it before God as an offering. Embracing what God does for you is the best thing you can do for him. Don't become so well adjusted to your culture that you fit into it without even thinking. Instead, fix your attention on God. You'll be changed from the inside out. Readily recognize what he wants from you, and quickly respond to it. Unlike the culture around you, always dragging you down to its level of immaturity, God brings the best out of you, develops well-formed maturity in you.

The New International Version of Romans 12:2 couches the idea differently: "Do not conform any longer to the pattern of this world, but be transformed by the renewing of your mind." This clearly tells us that we don't need to be molded into the shape the world offers. The world offers us lies about what we need to look like and act like in order to be valuable.

God offers a solution! Be changed by renewing your thoughts with things that are truthful and healthy. That will take some guidance from others and lots of practice. But the old statement "garbage in, garbage out," remains true. To recover, you need to replace the garbage of lies that Satan has used against you with the truth of God's unconditional love and acceptance of you.

When I speak at women's retreats, I often ask the crowd, "How many of you want to be mature women of God?" I've never yet found a woman who did not raise her hand. I want to be mature too. I just don't always volunteer to go through the process of maturing because it is often uncomfortable or even painful.

But God asks us to step out of our comfort zone, take His hand, and trust Him to be in control of growing us up into His likeness. It may hurt at times, but holding back and remaining immature in our addictions brings much more pain. Maturity is a pain that leads to a positive reward, whereas immaturity brings about pain that keeps us trapped in lies and bondage.

Recovery cannot begin until you admit that there is a problem. In therapy, I tell the compulsive overeaters and bulimics that as long as they stuff food, they are stuffing their feelings. So, learning to identify emotions and deal with them honestly represents the best place to start the recovery process. It can be like learning a foreign language to some people, but it is well worth the effort!

Being honest with yourself must be the first step. Then, find competent individual and group therapy because that is often the only place where women with eating disorders feel safe enough to honestly express themselves. Therapy is also important because of the life-threatening physical problems eating disorders sometimes cause.

If you struggle with this type of addiction, please seek out a counselor who specializes in eating disorders. There are many root issues that have led to the addiction, and you will need insight and guidance to face these. However, with help you can learn to identify your hidden emotions and deal with your anger, grief, and losses.

Do you ever remember feeling so ashamed of something that you dropped your head and stared at your feet? I can remember doing this when my mother confronted my disobedience during childhood. I wishfully thought if I didn't look up, maybe the problem would vanish and go away. I was so ashamed of what I had done that I wanted to avoid eye contact.

In the same way, you may feel trapped by an eating disorder or know someone who is. Many times I have counseled women struggling in this area who sit down in my office and never look up. They feel too ashamed to look at me. God wants you to be able to look up without any shame over who you are or what you've done.

Psalm 3:3 says,

> You are a shield around me O LORD; you bestow
> glory on me and lift up my head.

It blesses me to picture God putting His tender hand under the chin of a hurting woman, and gently lifting up her face as He removes the shame and replaces it with something glorious—the freedom to look up without shame! What a precious gift!

God lovingly wants to offer you the freedom to lift your head and look up as a wonderful, mature woman of God. You no longer need to feel frightened and out of control. Share your story honestly with someone and begin the process of coming out of your shame.

nine

LOSING AT LOVE:
THE CRUSHING BLOW OF DIVORCE

I will repay you for the years the locusts have eaten. . . .
You will have plenty to eat, until you are full,
and you will praise the name of the LORD your God,
who has worked wonders for you; . . .
Then you will know . . . that I am the LORD your God,
and that there is no other;
never again will my people be shamed.
JOEL 2:25-27

Whenever I plan a vacation, I look forward to it for months! I get on the Internet and find out all sorts of information about the area where we will go. I make lots of phone calls to find the perfect place to stay at the best prices. I research to make certain we don't miss a single attraction that the area has to offer, and I find all the well-known restaurants. Most people I know are the same way about their yearly getaway. It only lasts for a few days, so they want to make certain they get the most out of it.

It seems that many of us put more time and energy into learning about the site of our next vacation than we ever spend on learning how to be married or be a parent.

People rush into marriage with no preparation, then wonder why they are having such a difficult time with someone they thought they loved.

I was in the sixth grade before I ever knew someone whose parents were going through a divorce. This year, my daughter Elisabeth entered kindergarten and has already met children whose parents are divorced. Unfortunately, since no-fault divorce was made law in 1972, it has become an easy and common way to get out of a marriage. Instead of reciting the traditional wedding vows, which say, "Till death do us part," some now say, "As long as we both shall love."

Truth is, all marriages take hard work and commitment. Marriages that stay happy and healthy are marriages that have been nurtured. Anyone who has been married would agree that there are days when you don't feel very loving toward each other. Yet, the moment some couples hit rocky times they begin to ask, "Are we really right for each other?"

This question comes from believing the lie that there is only one person in the world with whom we could "live happily ever after." When we aren't happy, we fall into Satan's lie that says, "If this takes hard work, I must have married the wrong person. I should get out of this marriage and look for the perfect mate." But hard times can point out the flaws that need to be addressed in our own personalities.

I was twenty-six years old when I married David, and believe me, I was set in my ways! I had no idea how selfish I was until I had to live with David every day and take his feelings and opinions into consideration. I didn't enjoy learning that my way wasn't the only way or the right way to do things. Nonetheless, God has used our marriage to teach me to be a more giving person.

Proverbs 27:17 says, "As iron sharpens iron, so one man sharpens another." Marriage helps expose the areas of our lives that need to be addressed and changed. That process can be painful. So, if your marriage demands hard work, God has some things to teach you through it. Divorce may seem like a quick fix, but you will carry the same unresolved problems straight into the next marriage.

Jennifer married young in order to get away from home. She thought that anything would be better than living with her parents, so she got married a month after her high school graduation to a man she had only known for six months. It didn't take her long to figure out that her husband Jeff had a gambling problem. Why hadn't she seen this before? He used to joke with his buddies about betting on football games, but she had never really paid attention.

Now, he was often out overnight and never called to tell her where he was or when he would be home. She had to hide money out of her paycheck in order to make ends meet. The fighting escalated as she confronted him about not having enough money to meet their daily needs and living expenses because of his continual gambling.

After two years, their conflict intensified to include pushing and eventually hitting. Jennifer knew it was time to leave, but she felt so ashamed. No one in her family had ever divorced. If she left Jeff, she feared that people would label her a failure. So she begged Jeff to change and go to marriage counseling with her. Jeff laughed in her face and said that if she wouldn't file for a divorce, he would.

Now, twelve years later, Jennifer lives in a different state, has married another man, and has three precious children. She and her husband Tony share a loving relationship and remain active in their local church. But Jennifer lives with a nauseating fear in the pit of her stomach that someone will find out about her divorce from Jeff.

What if the women in her church group find out that she has been divorced? Will they treat her differently? Jennifer and Tony agreed long ago to keep the past a secret when they moved. Yet, Jennifer still worries. Should she explain her past to their children or try to pretend that it never really happened? What if someone in her family slips while visiting and says something about her first marriage? Jennifer makes herself sick when she imagines the past catching up with her.

No matter the circumstances of divorce, people end up wounded because they have broken a holy union that God ordained. Two people becoming one means that the two cleave together so closely that they cannot be separated without doing damage to each.

Equals Attract

Generational sin affects relationship choices. We are influenced by the family we grew up in, even when we are not aware of its patterns. For instance, women who grew up with an emotionally or physically distant father typically feel hungry for male attention. This neediness can lead her to getting involved in some very painful relationships as she seeks to fill the void in her heart for male approval.

In *Reclaiming Your Inner Child*, Ken Parker writes,

> A daughter may be profoundly affected by an emotionally distant father. She may grow up either avoiding all males or having relationships with several male partners, seeking male validation. Both situations tend to produce an approach-avoidance pattern. A woman will become deeply involved with men very quickly and then fearing rejection, will either break off the relationship or cling even tighter. Either way, she may become codependently involved with this other person.[1]

One of my college professors once said, "It's not so much about finding the right person as it is *being* the right person." I didn't understand his statement then the way I do now. I thought there was this perfect knight in shining armor that was going to come along and complete me—make my life perfect. I didn't realize that if you want to marry a prince, you need to be a princess.

Consider another reality check—we are each unconsciously attracted to people who are equal to us in being emotionally healthy or unhealthy. Simply put, we unconsciously choose a partner who lives at our own level of dysfunction. We are drawn to people who either need us to take care of them or are willing to rescue and care for us.

For instance, what emotionally healthy man searches for a bulimic woman when he looks for a marriage partner? Likewise, what woman with healthy respect and self-esteem searches for the most narcissistic, self-centered man she can find to spend the rest of her life with?

The person who marries the depressed person, the alcoholic, the gambler, the anorectic, and so on may appear stable. But internally, this person is motivated by a codependent need to rescue, fix, and control. In my profession, we call the person with the visible problem the "identified patient" in the family system. It's easy to focus on this one person and say that the other partner is healthy because his issues aren't so noticeable. However, his issues are just harder to detect or are more socially acceptable. For instance, he may be a workaholic or someone blinded by denial, but both partners are equally unhealthy or else they wouldn't be attracted to each other.

A Broken Union

Howard was a skillful furniture maker, and everyone in his trade admired him. One afternoon, Claire came into his shop to ask for advice on refinishing an antique chair. As they chatted, Claire noticed two beautiful pieces of mahogany on Howard's workbench. Eyeing them, she guessed that they would be a perfect replacement for two of the legs on the chair she was refinishing. So, when Howard excused himself to answer the telephone, she craftily unlocked a small side entry.

Around three A.M., Claire returned to the shop and sneaked in through the door she had secretly left open. She carried a small pin light to illuminate her way, moving slowly and carefully through the shop to keep from knocking anything over. In seconds, Claire got to the workbench, and the gleam of her light fell on the coveted wood.

Before scurrying out the door with them, she reasoned that Howard would not miss the pieces much. She hoped he would think they were misplaced. So she picked up the wood and for the first time realized that they were glued together. This would never work for her chair, and she felt angry that her efforts might not pay off with booty she could use. She struggled to pull the pieces apart and hoped that the glue had not set firmly. But it was no use.

Nevertheless, Claire slipped out the door, locked it behind her and carried the mahogany home. There, she took out a small chisel and began to try and pry the wood apart. In her frustration, she hit the chisel harder and heard a splitting sound as the pieces finally separated. She looked at the pieces in disgust as she realized that she had just ruined them both. The glue had set. And as the wood split, the original shape and beauty of the wood had been splintered apart.

So it is with marriage. God ordained that the two would become one flesh. When divorce occurs, the scars and damage of that separation are lifelong. Each person walks away, unable to recover parts of his or her heart and the trust that was given to the other. Each carries with them the ghostly remnants of their shared oneness.

Permanent Changes

Divorce involves an action that can never be undone. Even if there are no children involved, the partners are left with unanswered internal questions and feelings of failure.

"What did I do wrong?" they may ask. "Why didn't I see these problems before we got married? How could I have made it work? How in the world did I pick someone so much like my father?" They may wonder what other people think of them and feel uncomfortable around people who know about their former marriage.

Consider what Robert McGee describes in *The Search for Significance*:

> We all have compelling needs for love, acceptance, and purpose, and we will go to virtually any lengths to have those needs met. Many of us have become masters at "playing the game" to be successful and win the approval of others. Others, however, have failed often enough and experienced the pain of disapproval often enough that they have given up, withdrawing into a shell of hurt, numbness or depression.[2]

Often people lose friends because of a divorce. If they had other "couple" friends, the situation is often uncomfortable after the divorce, and each may feel like the "fifth wheel" at social gatherings because he or she is now the only one who isn't married. They may also lose friends as those friends pick sides among the couple and leave the other one out.

"For me, [divorce] was harder than a death," Hannah explained. "With a death, there is an ending. If I had been widowed, there would have been no scandal, no baggage to carry into the future. People would have offered me more comfort instead of avoiding me because they didn't know what to say. Also, if my husband died, I could grieve for him, but know that he was gone forever. Now, I grieve for him and for the oneness we shared together, but I know he is going on and living out his life with someone else. Sometimes I still feel like I hate him for the way he betrayed me."

Sarah also lamented the pain of divorce. When she discovered that her husband had been cheating on her, she experienced a profound sense of betrayal.

"I felt like everything I had ever believed in was a lie," she added. "Emotionally, I crumbled and felt unable to make any decisions about my life. It was a time when God seemed to wrap me in His arms of comfort. People were brought into my life to offer mentoring and to help me find a Christian counselor who could look at the situation objectively. Divorce was a time for me to 'cocoon' with God and let Him be my protector and the [One who can meet] my needs. I learned that God was right there with me to comfort me and love me."

Alli's husband left her with three young children. Until the day he left, she had no indication that anything was wrong with the marriage. She says the shock completely wiped out her self-esteem. For a while, she waited for Mike to return, but eventually realized that he had no plans to come home. She was heartbroken.

"The news of the divorce came crashing down on me because in my heart I still loved him," she recalled. "When the love for him continued, it was so lonely and painful. I finally had to ask God to please remove those feelings from me so that I didn't have to hurt so much each time he came to pick up the children. Eventually, God took those feelings away from me so that I could move forward in the healing process."

Priscilla also experienced a divorce and noticed that mutual friends she shared with her former husband treated her differently afterward. The wives didn't want her around their husbands when she became single again.

"I'd hear about birthday parties and cookouts after they occurred, but I was never invited. Not only did I lose my husband, I lost my support group," Priscilla explained. "I [also] find it interesting that if you go out to a bar and you haven't been divorced at least once, you don't fit in with the crowd. But if you go to church and you've been divorced, you are quickly made to feel that you don't fit in. There is certainly a double standard between the world and the church."

When Jennifer returned from a business trip, she found that her husband had taken half of their belongings and moved out. He left her a note that explained how he couldn't stay in the marriage anymore and would contact her soon. She felt shocked and devastated—especially because he left in a way that she perceived as unfair and cowardly.

In Jennifer's case, she knew that she and her husband were having problems. But she had no idea her husband planned to leave. Furthermore, he refused to disclose his reasons for leaving.

"There has never been any closure to that relationship," Jennifer confided. "It happened fifteen years ago, and I still have dreams about him where he will not talk to me or answer my questions. I struggle with trusting people. The thought of being hurt that badly again is more than I can take. I would rather be lonely than abandoned."

Edna said the hardest part of her divorce involved facing the holidays alone during that first year apart: "Suddenly, all of our family traditions were gone. I had to divide time with the children and let them spend half their time with their father. Letting them go that first Christmas afternoon was one of the saddest moments of my life. I sat in the floor in front of the Christmas tree and wept for hours. It seemed that all of my dreams for a happy family had been shattered. All I knew to do was cry out to the Lord with my broken heart."

When Amanda went through a divorce, members of her church rushed to support her. She and her husband had been active in that community, yet it became common knowledge that he had left her for another woman. Amanda felt strengthened by the love she was shown during that painful trial. Then, a few years later, she found herself sexually involved with a man she was dating. She admits that she made unhealthy choices out of neediness and the fear that she would never be loved again.

Ultimately, the same group that supported her during her divorce turned on her when they found out she was sleeping with someone. The pastor even asked her to leave the church. Suddenly, her support system was gone. Losing her friends was as painful to her as losing her husband through the divorce. Now, she says she deliberately stays on the periphery at any church she attends.

"Getting involved is just too risky," she revealed. "There is a need to hide my past from church members because no matter what I say, they will judge me. There is simply too much to be ashamed of in the church. You don't know who other people really are or what they are struggling with. I don't ever want to be involved enough to get hurt again."

The Difficulty of Forgiveness

If you have gone through a divorce, you fit into one of three categories. In the first, your husband wanted the divorce, and you were deeply hurt. In the second, you were the one who instigated the divorce. In the third, you and your husband both agreed to the divorce. Regardless of your situation, divorce damages hearts. It generally requires both parties to go through the process of forgiveness, which can be challenging.

> We find some perverse joy in licking old wounds. We return to the hurts again and again, reliving them in a movie we play in the theaters of our minds . . . a movie in which we are the stars. We see ourselves abused, wronged—but oh so right. Every time we play this movie in our imagination, we hear again what each person said or didn't say, what was done and how it was done. We cling to our memories because in our darkened minds, we believe that if we forget, the one who hurt us may go free! . . . Bitterness arises from the

belief that the person who hurt us owes us and must somehow pay us back.[3]

Many of my divorced clients explain that they've been hurt so many times in romantic relationships that they will make sure they are never hurt again. Every time they got hurt, they added another brick to their emotional wall of protection.

Their anger may guard them from the hurt of rejection, but the anger also walls them off from the very intimacy that God created them to need with Him and others. Still, these women have promised themselves that no one will ever control them again. It is true that they can now avoid vulnerability and the hurt of rejection, but they will suffer with a deep loneliness that can be just as painful.

> There are those who clutch to resentment like it were a treasure of great worth. This is foolishness. The question to be asked is not how badly we were wronged, but what are we profited by our unforgiveness?[4]

> To love at all is to be vulnerable. Love anything and your heart will certainly be wrung and possibly broken. If you want to make sure of keeping it intact, you must give your heart to no one. . . . Wrap it carefully round with hobbies and little luxuries; avoid all entanglements; lock it up safe in the casket or coffin of your selfishness. But in that casket—safe, dark, motionless, airless—it will change. It will not be broken; it will become unbreakable, impenetrable, irredeemable.[5]

Forgiveness is difficult, but necessary if you want to move forward in life. After all, maintaining a bitter spirit can cause great damage in your life. Since Jesus is the ultimate forgiver, we can rely on Him as a role model. He is the only one who both understands the depth of your bitterness and your ability to forgive with His help.

A Time to Consider

If you are married and considering divorce, I urge you to save the marriage. Keep in mind that children are always damaged by divorce, and their little lives should always be our first unselfish consideration. There are many excellent Christian marriage counselors who can offer guidance and help for rebuilding damaged relationships. If you don't know how to find one, talk with a local pastor and see who he recommends.

I believe that in some cases divorce is necessary and biblical. For instance, I would never ask any woman to stay with a physically violent man, a drug addict, an active alcoholic, or an unrepentant adulterer. But too often, people leave a marriage without even trying to resolve the conflicts. In fact, working through conflict matures both partners and helps them bond. Above all else, it is what God tells us to do in obedience to Him.

Almost everyone has been touched by divorce in one way or another. Maybe you have a close friend or sibling who has gone through a divorce and needed your support during that painful time of change. Others are the product of divorced parents, and may still carry the scars of that broken marriage.

Incidentally, adult children of divorce have a higher rate of divorce than adults who come from intact marriages. Part of the problem is that they tend to choose more unstable partners and have fewer reservations about getting out when the going gets tough. They reason that if it was okay for their parents, it's okay for them.

Offspring of divorced parents also experience more problems with intimacy and trust. Some avoid relationships because they think that if their parents were miserable failures in marriage, they probably will be too. If your parents divorced, you may also struggle with the shame of feeling that you were somehow responsible. But children are never powerful enough to be responsible for the actions of adults! Even if one or both parents placed blame on you, the divorce was their decision and was not about you.

God Is the Ultimate Provider

When God instructed Moses to lead the children of Israel out of Egypt and into the Promised Land, he was concerned with how he would explain God's leading to the people.

"Who shall I say has sent me?" Moses asked.

"I AM WHO I AM," God replied. "Thus, you shall say to the children of Israel, 'I AM has sent me to you'" (Exodus 3:14).

I get excited about that verse because I see that God still says that to us today. When we are discouraged, rejected, and hurting, we can remember that God is still the great "I AM." We can fill in the blanks of what we need God to be for us at that moment—"I AM" your comforter, encourager, husband, friend, confidant, strength, healer, supporter, guide, and loving Heavenly Father. "I AM" the one who loves you more than any other. "I AM" your protector and redeemer. "I AM" the one who delivers you out of all your fears and turns your sorrow into joy.

God has the awesome ability to be what we need, when we need it. He shows concern for all of our feelings and needs, and He knows us intimately. Furthermore, God is perfect, and His abilities are limitless and multifaceted. People may have let us down, but God remains trustworthy and will never fail us. We can place our confidence in His ability and desire to take care of us.

Psalm 30:11-12 reveals what God will do as we cling to Him: "You turned my wailing into dancing; you removed my sackcloth and clothed me with joy, that my heart may sing to you and not be silent. O LORD my God, I will give you thanks forever."

Part 3

A Plan of Hope
and Glory

ten

DEƧIRED BY GOD:
YOU ARE A WOMAN OF GREAT VALUE

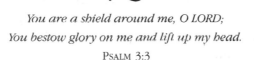

You are a shield around me, O LORD;
You bestow glory on me and lift up my head.
PSALM 3:3

Linda struggled to hide her feelings of inferiority and insecurity through perfectionism. She tried hard to maintain the appearance of a perfect marriage, perfect children, a perfectly immaculate home, and a perfectly fulfilling social calendar. She got so wrapped up in performing for her worth and identity that she dared not drop the superwoman persona for fear of disappointing others.

In addition to appearing invincible, Linda also wanted to be popular with everyone. So, she conformed to who she thought others wanted her to be. While jumping through all these hoops, she never appreciated that God gave her this thirst for self-worth and approval nor that God was the only one who could meet those deeply felt needs.

If you feel like Linda, I have exciting news for you! God says that each one of us is a woman of great value—just as we are, regardless of our track record of both accomplishments and failures. Each of us has a priceless value in the eyes of Christ. But if that's the case, then how did so many of us lose sight of that value?

Today, mainstream American society ties value to external issues such as the success of your children, the size of your home, the class of your friends, the dollar amount of your paycheck, the accomplishments of your husband, and your achievements, not to mention the quality of your looks.

Flip on the tube, and it will bombard you with images of the ideal female look—youthful women who wear a size four, have flawless skin, and dazzling, straight, white teeth. It's easy to feel inferior as women when we constantly view these images of perfection. Thank goodness God has other ideas about our worth.

> When Christ told His disciples, "You shall know the truth and the truth shall set you free" (John 8:32), He wasn't referring only to an intellectual assent to the truth. He was referring to the application of truth in the most basic issues of life: our goals, our motives, and our sense of self-worth.
>
> Unfortunately, many of us give only lip service to the powerful truths of the Scriptures without allowing them to radically affect the basis of our self-worth. Instead, we continue to seek our security and purpose from the world's sources: personal success, status, beauty, wealth, and the approval of others. These may fulfill for a short time, but soon they lead to a sense of urgency to succeed and be approved again.[1]

In the Garden of Eden before the Fall, Adam and Eve never struggled with self-worth. God met all their needs—physical, intellectual, emotional, and of course, spiritual. And they enjoyed sweet fellowship with each other and with God. This close relationship with God gave them a deep and secure sense of self-worth because they clearly understood how very much He loved and cherished them.

However, when Adam and Eve abandoned their relationship with God out of pride and rebellion, they lost that sense and instead began feeling shame, worthlessness, emptiness, and so forth. Like them, we have tried hiding from God instead of running to Him with these very same issues. In fact, some use an exorbitant amount of energy every day for years in order to hide who they really are, and how they really feel, from God and others.

I Must Have Everyone's Love and Approval

As kids growing up in Alabama, my brother Wayne and I used to catch little lizards called chameleons. The chameleon is a very interesting creature. For self-protection, he has the ability to change skin color and fit into his current environment. If you place him in a jar with bright green pine straw, you can watch the pigment change as he slowly turns to the exact shade of green. Take him out and place him on brown dead leaves, and soon he will be a matching shade of brown. God has given him these changing pigments in order to protect him from predators as he blends into his surroundings.

Many of us try hard to be "social chameleons." We want so desperately to be accepted by others that we will try to fit in at any cost. When we are in the green group, we act green. When we are in the brown group, we act brown. And someone help us if we are ever exposed to people from both groups at the same time because we won't know how in the world to behave!

For instance, Linda was so desperate for approval that she avoided conflict at any cost. If someone seemed angry with her, she would say she was sorry—even when she knew that she hadn't done anything wrong. She would change what she wanted to do if she thought it would please someone else. No wonder she got so confused about who she was and what she thought.

The 20/60/20 Truth

A psychologist once underscored the futility of people-pleasing by explaining the 20/60/20 truth. He argued that twenty percent of the people you meet will immediately like you, sixty percent will not feel strongly one way or the other, and the remaining twenty percent will immediately not like you.

Makes sense, doesn't it? After all, you know when you've met a woman who is in your top twenty-percent. You feel an immediate chemistry with her, and you look forward to the next time you will see her again. Then, there's the gal who is in your bottom twenty-percent. You quickly feel a dislike for her personality. She irritates you more than someone who scrapes a fingernail on a chalkboard, and you silently hope that you never have to run into her again.

When you meet a woman in the other sixty percent, you note her neutrally. She makes neither a positive or negative impression. You may serve on a school committee with her or attend a Bible study group together, but she may be so quiet that you don't feel any more strongly about her for months. One day, it dawns on you that she is a very kind person, and that you like her. Or, you may eventually realize that she has a critical spirit, and you don't care to deepen your friendship.

All three responses are normal responses toward women and men alike because we all have different personality types, and no type is attractive to everyone. Furthermore, you would not want to have everyone's love and approval. If every woman you ever met wanted to be your best friend, you would feel overwhelmed.

For instance, you would receive hundreds of birthday cards, and you would feel obligated to find out when their birthdays were and make sure you returned a card to them. Your phone would never stop ringing with invitations to lunch, and the list goes on. When would you have time to develop genuine, deep friendships with any of them?

Yet, many women spend incredible amounts of time and energy believing the lie that they must have everyone's love and approval. We can become addicted to the approval of others and become upset or depressed when we don't get it.

When I shared the 20/60/20 Truth with my client Linda, the recovering superwoman, she started to smile and I saw a light bulb blink on in her eyes. She finally understood how hard she was working for approval that she could never attain and, in reality, would never want.

"You know, you're right, Cynthia. There are plenty of people that I don't really care for or want to spend time with," she reflected. "I need to accept that some people feel the same way about me no matter what I do. It would be a great relief to stop working so hard to get everyone to like me! As long as I know I'm treating everyone fairly, then I am going to try to stop worrying about what they think."

We must base our self-worth on who we are in Christ. Because that kind of worth is tied to the very nature of God, it never changes. Furthermore, after many years, I've finally learned that just because a person perceives me in one way doesn't make that perception true.

You may very well think I'm six feet tall, but that won't alter the fact that I am 5'6". There is a great freedom in knowing that as long as I allow God to control my life and develop me into His character, I don't need to worry about how other people interpret the way I live my life.

The Fundamentals

If you remain caught in the trap of people pleasing and striving to be superwoman, consider these fundamental truths. Each one underscores how acceptable and lovable you are to God—without ever lifting a finger.

GOD LOVES YOU

I have struggled with depression intermittently since childhood. However, it was not diagnosed and treated until my mid-twenties. So, I often believed that my painful emotions were related to my poor spiritual performance. I figured if I could just pray more, I could please God and overcome my pain.

In this way, I unwittingly based my belief system about God on a set of legalistic standards to which I could never measure up. Yet, I found my value in my performance—not God's love. Through the lenses of legalism, I saw God as distant and aloof. This perspective drove me to work harder and harder to somehow earn His approval.

With no joy at all, I would sit down to an hour's worth of quiet time and hope that it made God happy. Yet, deep within, I felt the hopelessness of knowing I could never be good enough or work hard enough to make God love me. I felt I could never please Him, and those thoughts pushed me deeper into my depression.

By my senior year of college, I had exhausted myself with this approach. But I hid behind an even higher wall of performance so I wouldn't appear to be spiritually immature. For instance, I forced myself to spend time alone with God each day, lead music every Thursday night at the Campus Crusade meeting, teach a Bible study each week for new believers, and participate in a Bible study group for mature leaders. Through it all, I was gritting my teeth and telling God, "I am going to make You love me!"

One day, I collapsed from all these efforts and felt like I wanted to die. Racked with weeping, I crawled into my bed in that tiny dorm room and fell into a restless sleep. The ringing telephone woke me and upon picking it up, I heard the soothing voice of one of my Christian friends. The tears began again as I told him how lost I felt and how my relationship with God seemed hopeless.

"Cynthia, you know so much about God in your head and so little about Him in your heart," he said after I had poured out all my pain.

"What do you mean I don't know God in my heart?" I responded in confusion. His response has been one of those "light bulb" experiences for me, and it stays deeply imprinted on my heart today.

"God loves you because it is an attribute of God to love you. In the same way that you can't change that you're female, God is loving, and He will never change that. He loves you with the same amount of love that He had for you ten years ago, and He will love you just the same in your future. God doesn't love you because you look like you have it all together in front of others, or because you teach Bible studies or spend a certain amount of time in prayer," he added. "You can't work to earn the love of God. If you never work another minute to serve God, His love for you will never change because the reason He loves you is based on who He is, not on what you do."

The greatest distance in the world is often the space between your heart and head. Sometimes you may clearly believe a fact in your head, but your actions and feelings show a completely different set of beliefs in your heart.

Have you come to a place where you want to know God with your whole heart? Do you want to feel peaceful, resting in the strength of God's unconditional love for you? Start by learning the truth about God's love for you! It has absolutely *nothing* to do with you. You can't work to earn it. You can't be good enough to receive it. It is a gift.

First John 4:9-10 says, "This is how God showed his love among us: He sent his one and only Son into the world that we might live through him. This is love: not that we loved God, but that he loved us and sent his Son as an atoning sacrifice for our sins."

I wasted lots of time and energy trying to figure out how to capture God's love. "God will show his love toward me like this," I mused. "If I am really, really good, if I get all my ducks in a row, if I make an A+ every time, then God will love me."

Of course, you know that I later learned God's true response: "No, Cynthia. While you were still filthy and rotten and decaying in your sin, I had compassion on you and loved you so much that I gave everything for you. I gave up my precious Son in order to restore my relationship with you."

1 John 3:1 says, "How great is the love the Father has lavished on us, that we should be called children of God!" I don't know about you, but I love presents! Once or twice I've been known to say, "Oh, you shouldn't have," or "This is really too much!" But I have never once turned down a gift. God stands before you today and offers you a gift. It may be free, but it is not cheap.

In fact it is the most extravagant gift ever offered because it was purchased by the offering of God's only Son, Jesus Christ. That's just how much God loves you and desires to be reconciled into a loving relationship with you. No matter who you are, where you've been, what you've done, or are currently doing, God offers you His free gift of love and salvation.

GOD REMEMBERS YOU

Isaiah 49:15-16 says, "Can a mother forget the baby at her breast and have no compassion on the child she has borne? Though she may forget, I will not forget you! See, I have engraved you on the palms of my hands; your walls are ever before me."

When I first read this passage several years ago, I was still a nursing mother. It was hard for me to understand, because I knew that I could certainly never forget to nurse my child. Then I realized that there have been many mothers who have abandoned their children instead of caring for them and meeting their needs. I realized that Isaiah is using the most intimate and nurturing of relationships to show that even a mother could neglect the needs of the infant who is totally dependent on her. Even a mother will abandon her own flesh and blood in some situations.

But though she could forget, God will *never* forget us—no matter what! One of the reasons God says He can't forget us is because He has engraved our name on the very palm of His hand!

As a high-school student, I remember writing phone numbers in the palm of my hand. I wrote them there because I knew I would have to see them later, and this ensured that I would remember them. There was one problem with that method of memory jogging. Ink wears off, washes off, and sweats off. It frustrated me to look down and find that a numeral was missing from the phone number.

But God promises that He can never forget about us because our name is engraved in the palm of His hand! Now if you know anything about engraving, it does not wash off. It's permanent. Can you imagine what would happen if you had something engraved on your palm? How many times do you think you would see it as you used your hands during the day? It would be a constant reminder to you.

God says He thinks about you *constantly* because your name is always in front of Him. Every time God moves His hands, He sees your name and thinks loving thoughts about you as His precious child. All day and all night, He tenderly remembers how much He loves you. How very important we must be to the most High God, the Creator of the universe.

GOD APPRECIATES DETAILS

One of my favorite verses is Matthew 10:29-31: "Are not two sparrows sold for a penny? Yet not one of them will fall to the ground apart from the will of your Father. And even the very hairs of your head are all numbered. So don't be afraid; you are worth more than many sparrows."

Did you know that God, the Creator of the universe, the Creator of you, has such an intimate interest in your life that He knows the number of hairs you pulled into your brush this morning and the number that stayed on your head? Whether you succeed at getting the attention of others or not, that image shows me that God notices us—even in terms of minutia.

A few weeks ago, we attended our daughter's soccer game. I had a sinus headache, so I had taken an antihistamine. During the game, I kept feeling a strange sensation on one little spot on my scalp. I have taken medications in the past that caused my scalp to tingle, so I ignored it. Later, in the car on the way home, I felt it again. I wondered why the medication was only bothering one nerve, but I again ignored it.

When we arrived, I decided to lie down for a while. Immediately, I felt a stinging in that spot, so I reached into my hair and pulled out a bug the size of a dime. There was quite a bit of screaming and dancing around on my part as I made sure that bug suffered through death by smashing!

My war dance tickled my husband so much that he could not stop laughing. And tears flooded the eyes of my children as they giggled and called me a jumping frog. When David finally caught his breath, he said, "Only you have thick enough hair to have a bug roosting around in there for an hour and not even know it!"

"That's okay," I responded. "God knew it was in there the whole time, and He even knew it was perching on hair number 2,562!"

GOD SOLVES SIN

What a relief! What a joy to know that God never leaves us without a solution for our sins. We can never come to a place where His forgiveness runs out. 1 John 1:9 says, "If we confess our sins, he is faithful and just and will forgive our sins and purify us from *all* unrighteousness" (emphasis mine).

This is a contract, a covenant that God makes with us. If you do this, He'll do that. If you confess, He forgives. And the amazing thing is that when He forgives us, He forgets our sin. He casts that sin into the sea of His forgetfulness. God remembers it no more. After you have repented and asked God to forgive you, if you go back and talk to God about it, it's as if He says, "What sin?"

You may have had parents or a spouse who kept a list of all your sins and reminded you of them in order to manipulate you, but God will never treat you that way. If you ever hear from that sin again, it will not be from God, but from Satan.

Psalm 103:10-12 says, "He does not treat us as our sins deserve or repay us according to our iniquities. For as high as the heavens are above the earth, so great is his love for those who fear him; as far as the east is from the west, so far has he removed our transgressions from us."

Unlike God, we often get stuck remembering the past and feel shame and guilt over our mistakes. In this way, we allow Satan to use the past to keep us in bondage to the lie that God could never forgive us for such horrible behavior. Satan whispers, "You've hurt too many other people for God to forgive you."

Eugene Peterson makes God's plan clear in *The Message* by putting Romans 6 into contemporary language:

> When Jesus died, He took sin down with him, but alive he brings God down to us. From now on, think of it this way: Sin speaks a dead language that means nothing to you. God speaks your mother tongue, and you hang on every word. You are dead to sin and alive to God. That's what Jesus did.
>
> That means you must not give sin a vote in the way you conduct your lives. Don't give it the time of day. Don't even run little errands that are connected with that old way of life. Throw yourself whole-heartedly and full time—remember, you've been raised from the dead!—into God's way of doing things. Sin can't tell you how to live. After all, you're not living under that old tyranny any longer. You're living in the freedom of God.

Sin is no longer our master because we are living under God's incredible grace.

> You dear children, are from God and have overcome
> them, because the one who is in you is greater than
> the one who is in the world. (1 John 4:4)

The best advertising for anything is a satisfied customer. When you go to a restaurant where the food is terrific, you tell your friends about it and make plans to eat there again soon. Our assignment as God's forgiven people is to be His witness that there is a solution to sin, guilt, and shame. When people see the peace in our own lives, they will be drawn in and want to know what makes us different from them. It gives us a wonderful opportunity to share with them the freedom and truth that God has provided a solution for all of our sins.

GOD GIVES GRACE

There is great news! Shout for joy! The cross of Christ has bridged the Grand Canyon created by sin, and we never need to be alone again. Nor do we need to try to push through life on our own strength. That is the beauty of understanding God's amazing grace. Remember this truth: Our value is not in who we are, but in *whose* we are.

eleven

HEALING LOVE:
GOD'S PLAN OF GRACE

*"But while he was still a long way off, his father saw him and
was filled with compassion for him; he ran to his son, threw his
arms around him and kissed him. The son said to him, 'Father,
I have sinned against heaven and against you. I am no longer
worthy to be called your son.' But the father said to his
servants, 'Quick! Bring the best robe and put it on him. Put a
ring on his finger and sandals on his feet. Bring the fattened
calf and kill it. Let's have a feast and celebrate. For this son of
mine was dead and is alive again; he was lost and is found.'
So they began to celebrate."*
LUKE 15:20-24

William Berry was a wealthy oilman who got his start working in the oil fields at age thirteen. He never finished his
formal education, but he had grown over the years into a wise
businessman. He worked his way up from the bottom, and was
now the owner and CEO of a large oil company in Dallas.

His son Dave worked hard to learn all he could about his
father's business, but his daughter Jesse never could seem to get
her act together. One evening, when William asked about her

plans for a summer job, she became angry.

"I don't plan to do anything this summer!" yelled the teen. "I wish you were dead so I could have my half of the inheritance and do whatever I please with my own life!" William was deeply hurt by his daughter's remarks, but he responded in a way that surprised her.

"Jesse, you don't have to wish me dead. I will give you your inheritance tomorrow morning," he said. The next day after receiving her money, Jesse felt ecstatic! She headed to the local Porsche dealer and bought the most expensive car on the lot. Then, she zoomed off to Las Vegas to have some fun.

For the next two years, Jesse was the hit of Vegas. People recognized her car and waved as they saw her cruising the casino strip with a different guy every night. Typically, she moved in big groups—it seemed that everyone wanted to spend time with her to get in on some of the big bucks she threw around so freely. She especially liked mixing with the showgirls because they didn't judge her for her lack of education.

Whatever her company, Jesse partied with alcohol and drugs all night and slept all day at the penthouse suite she leased at one of the grand hotels. She and her entourage started most evenings by gambling at one of the ritziest casinos. The casino owners knew that young Jesse was a multi-millionaire, so they offered her a line of credit when she gambled.

Jesse had no idea how to manage her money. She gambled and drugged her way into tremendous debt before she even knew it. And as she entered her favorite casino one night, the bouncers took her to a room in the back. The owner made it clear that he wanted the line of credit repaid immediately.

Jesse's throat was so dry she couldn't swallow. All she could think about was finding her dealer to get some cocaine so this would all just go away. Jesse promised she would get the money, but the owner knew the bank had closed her account. After punching her in the face a few times, they took her jewelry and her purse. Then they threw Jesse out back into an alley.

She was bleeding out her nose and the corner of her mouth. One of her eyes was swollen shut, and she could feel the jagged edge on her broken front tooth. It took her quite a while to stand up and stumble to the parking lot. Her red Porsche had already been repossessed, and none of her "friends" had shown up to support her. Now that her money was gone, everyone who followed her night after night was gone too. Jesse soon staggered down the street to the hotel where she lived. But when she tried to enter, the doorman stopped her.

"You can't come in here." he said, stepping in front of her.

"What do you mean I can't come in here?" she cried. "I live here! All of my things are here!"

"Not anymore you don't live here." he smirked. "Seems Miss High and Mighty ran up too many bills. Your things will be sold at auction to repay your debt."

Surely this couldn't be happening to her! Just yesterday, her life had been one big party! Dismayed, Jesse found a public fountain and cleaned herself up a bit. She had no idea what to do for money or food, and for the next two nights she slept on a park bench. Finally, she decided she had no other choice except to join the ranks of the prostitutes that she used to ridicule. She began to sell her body in order to get money for food and drugs. As long as she could stay high, she didn't have to think much about the wretched life she was living.

One night, a pimp beat her up for moving in on the territory of one of his girls. After the beating, her health started to fail. When the cooler winter weather set in, she developed a constant, painful cough. And she couldn't make any money because no one wanted a coughing, sick prostitute. She began to sleep on the streets again and rummage for food in the garbage cans behind restaurants. The withdrawal from her drug addiction was horrible. Her body was wracked with pain.

One night, as she lay huddled on a park bench trying to keep warm, she vaguely remembered her home in Dallas. As she thought more about the ranch, she recalled how it was always safe and warm there. Even the workers in her father's oil fields and his ranch hands had warm places to sleep and plenty to eat. His hired help lived a better life than she.

"But I can't go home," she mused. "I humiliated my father in front of all of his friends. I said I wished he were dead. I don't know if he could ever forgive me." Yet, try as she might, she couldn't put the thoughts of home out of her mind.

"What a waste I've made of my life!" she finally conceded. "I had everything, and I threw it all away in search of a good time. But it wasn't a good time. People only pretended to love me in order to get my money. They used me just like I used my dad. How could I have been so foolish? I've made such a mess of my life. I am so ashamed of what I've done. My father can probably never forgive me. But I have to at least try. There's nothing left for me to do except go home."

Her body ached as the cough grew worse. Finally, in desperation she decided to return and apologize. She figured that if she begged him, he might hire her on as a ranch hand. At least that way she would have a place to live and food to eat. So, Jesse gathered all she owned in her backpack and hitchhiked toward Texas. Three days later, she arrived in Dallas—sweaty, tired, and nervous.

"Maybe I shouldn't have come back," she thought. "What if Dad yells at me and tells me to leave? I certainly deserve that. But, I may as well go find out. What other choices do I have? More than anything, I just want him to know that I'm sorry for all I've done wrong."

Her last ride dropped her off about a mile from the ranch, and as she slowly walked down the road, she silently rehearsed what she needed to say. Suddenly, she heard someone yelling and looked up to see her father running down the road toward her. All of the ranch hands turned to watch their boss running in humility to the daughter they had all called a whore.

For a moment, Jesse panicked. Was he screaming for her to leave? No! He was running with his arms wide open.

"Jesse is home!" he shouted. "She's alive! I thought you were dead, but you are safe at last!" When William reached her, there were tears streaming down his cheeks. He wrapped his arms around her, lifted her off the ground and spun her around with excitement.

"Daddy, I'm sorry, I was . . . " she tried to speak.

"Hush child," he responded. "None of that matters now. I love you, and whatever you've done is in the past. What matters is that you are home safely! This is the happiest day of my life! Let's go up to the house." He kept his arm around her even though she stank for need of a bath.

"Sweetheart, why are you shaking so much?" he asked with compassion.

"Daddy, I've gotten myself into a lot of trouble," she confessed. "I need a drug rehab program."

"We will take care of that tomorrow morning. But tonight, we are going to celebrate!" her dad replied tenderly as he pushed her greasy hair out of her eyes. "Why don't you go to the kitchen and get something to eat? Then, I bet you'd like to take a nice hot shower." He started calling out orders to the workers nearby. "Call the caterer! Tell them we are having a party tonight! Make sure it's the best party they have ever done! Hire a band! Call all of our neighbors and friends and tell them to come and celebrate that Jesse is home at last!"

God is like this loving, forgiving father. We can make the biggest mess of our lives while we try to do things our own way. We can embarrass Him, mock His name, and hurt others and ourselves. Yet, He patiently waits for us to come home. And when we finally do come home, He humbles Himself by running to meet us.

Can you imagine the God who set the moon and stars in place dropping everything to run to you, to embrace you and bring you home? He doesn't wait until we clean up our act, until we beg long and hard enough for forgiveness. In fact, He knows we can never clean up by ourselves. We are in desperate need of help, so He freely gives forgiveness to His needy and hurting children, like only a loving Heavenly Father can. He wipes the slate clean with the blood of Christ. Through His grace, He meets us right where we are and rejoices that we have come home at last!

Psalm 103:8,10-14 says, "The LORD is compassionate and gracious, slow to anger, abounding in love. He does not treat us as our sins deserve or repay us according to our iniquities. For as high as the heavens are above the earth, so great is his love for those who fear him; as far as the east is from the west, so far has he removed our transgression from us. As a father has compassion on his children, so the LORD has compassion on those who fear him; for he knows how we are formed, he remembers that we are dust."

God is tenderhearted toward us. He knows exactly how He created us from dust, and He knows that we are weak and needy people. Furthermore, from the moment that Adam and Eve sinned against God, He began to plan a way to bring us back into a close, restored relationship with Him. He gave us His very best when he sent the Lord Jesus to live in the flesh and blood body of a human being. He allowed Jesus to be the perfect lamb that was sacrificed to take away our sins. God knew that on our own, we could never restore our relationship with Him. So, He did all the work for us.

Ephesians 2:8-10 says, "For it is by grace you have been saved, through faith—and this not from yourselves, it is the gift of God—not by works, so that no one can boast. For we are God's workmanship, created in Christ Jesus to do good works, which God prepared in advance for us to do."

These verses underscore that we can never please God on our own. If we could, then we would all go around bragging about how wonderful we are, and we would completely forget that God did the work. Reconciliation with God through His grace represents a tremendous gift that we don't deserve and could *never* earn.

God's Workmanship

I once had a friend who was a talented wood carver, and I loved to watch him use his pocketknife to whittle a block of wood into something new. Occasionally, he stopped to sharpen his knife, but he returned to the wood with a sense of purpose and joy.

I don't have much artistic ability in that area, so watching him craft the wood fascinated me. When I asked him how he could take a block of wood and end up with a beautiful bird, he explained that he always kept a picture of the bird he desired to create in his mind's eye. He worked to whittle away anything that did not resemble the bird he pictured.

Sometimes we are like that block of wood. God looks at our lives, and He desires to make us into the image of Jesus Christ. So, He has a picture of what He wants us to look like. With that in mind, He begins to carve away the things in our lives that don't look like Jesus. The only problem is, we aren't a block of wood. We have feelings and opinions of our own about this process. When He cuts off a rough edge, we protest.

"Hey, what are You doing?" we holler. "I liked that area of my life! I wasn't ready to give that up yet." Sometimes we hinder the process by walking away or rebelling against His will. I've been known to pray this immature prayer: "God please make me like You, but please don't let it hurt." The good news is that God never takes away anything that is positive and Christlike, only those things that hinder us from growing into maturity.

COMING AROUND AGAIN

Sometimes, I have to learn this lesson again and again as was the case when God recently removed another rough edge in my life. In the weariness of struggling with my depression, I had become angry with Him. I had started to tell God that if He really loved me, He would heal me. When the healing did not come, I felt even angrier and accused Him of not truly loving me.

That anger caused a "root of bitterness" in my heart toward God. I didn't feel like praying to a God who was withholding healing from me. I missed our intimate relationship, but I bought into the lie that I couldn't trust Him anyway since He wouldn't give me what I wanted. One day, a friend asked me what would happen if I "embraced" my depression.

"You must be kidding," I cynically laughed. "If I embraced my depression, then that means I would stop fighting it. I would be even more depressed. I might drown in it!" Others had even told me to be thankful for the depression, and I would feel angry and lash out.

"You don't understand depression if you think somehow I can be thankful for this pain!" I'd retort. "You've obviously never been in the abyss of depression, or you would know that it is hell on earth."

Out of frustration, I took matters into my own hands. If God wouldn't give me miraculous healing, then maybe a doctor could. So, I headed to the Mayo Clinic in Rochester, Minnesota—the Mecca of medical research. Surely doctors there would have some type of cutting-edge technology that would heal me. But God had other plans! My dear friend Patty drove from Iowa to stay with me at Mayo. After two days together, she lovingly confronted me with the truth about what she saw in my life.

"Cynthia, you are believing a lie, and it has put you in bondage. In your anger, you have let go of knowing that God loves you no matter what you go through or how you feel." She was right. There was a lot of weeping on my part that night, but God was starting to break down the barriers that were keeping us apart. The wonderful lesson that I learned in college about the unchanging love of God had been pulled slowly away from me as I focused on my depression and blamed God for it. Thank goodness that because of His grace, He didn't give up on me. Instead, He provided a special friend to speak the truth to me in love.

That conversation launched a new process. For instance, after I returned home, I shared how I was feeling with another friend who has also struggled with depression. God had me ready to hear what she had to say.

"It's not wrong to be weak," she shared. "It really is okay! What I've learned recently in the first beatitude is, 'Blessed are the poor in spirit, for theirs is the kingdom of heaven.' To be 'poor in spirit,' requires knowing that we are desperate for and dependent on the Lord's strength. What a hindrance human strength and self-sufficiency can be! How easily it makes us forget that whether we feel able or not, we are still needy people. So, if you're suffering in human weakness from a God-given tendency, shout 'Hallelujah!'"

"The other aspect of poorness in spirit is a humility, which would involve the acceptance of who and what God made us," she continued. "You mentioned that you're afraid that if you stop trying to get better, the darkness will overwhelm you. I wonder if the Lord is waiting for you to stop trying. Don't get me wrong. I'm all for fighting depression. To not fight would be to believe the lies. Fighting rejects the lies and replaces them with a corresponding truth from the Word of God. It's a principle that is so simple, yet so profound."

The truth finally broke through to my heart and my head at the same time. In the past, I had been able to acknowledge that God had used my depression since childhood to teach me many things. I could apply Romans 8:28 to the depression. I knew it had helped me develop a more compassionate heart as a counselor and that it helped me in my writing and speaking. My struggle with depression had also given me more compassion to share with others.

But I couldn't see anything positive about this struggle in the present. I felt it hindered me from being an energetic mommy and wife—that it kept me from having the drive to write faster or to develop friendships. But the truth remained. No matter what my circumstances and how much I understood them, God's love for me is still abundant and constant. I decided to trust once again that in my weakness, He always proves Himself strong.

For the first time in my life, I told God, "Thank You for making me just as I am. Thank You for the depression. I will trust You to teach me whatever You desire. Even if You never heal me, I will trust You."

Admittedly, those were difficult words to say! But later, a peace came into my heart. It has been such a comfort to be able to freely pray and fellowship with God again! I had allowed my anger to build a barrier between us and had bought into one of Satan's favorite lies that God doesn't really love me enough.

If you've bought into that same lie because of what you've done in the past or because of a current area of struggle, find hope and comfort in Hebrews 13:5-6: "For he has said, 'I will never leave you or forsake you.' So we can say with confidence, 'The Lord is my helper; I will not be afraid.'" (NRSV). God will never leave us, and His love for us never changes. I like the word "never" used in these verses. It means not at any time, no matter what we have done.

The world tells us that we must be strong to succeed. But God tells us we are in the right place when we are needy and weak because then we stop depending on ourselves and turn to Him to provide our strength! So, I repeat my friend's counsel to others who struggle. If you feel weak, that's great! You are now in the place to plunge into the unending grace and strength of God. You are right where God wants you to be. Stop fighting it and rest in His love for you. He desires to be the One who meets your needs.

WOMEN OF GRACE

Historically, God has chosen to use broken, weak, sinful people to serve Him and fulfill His plans. Matthew 1 outlines Christ's lineage and includes the names of four women because each one had a life marked by grace.

Tamar, daughter of King David, suffered an incestuous rape by her brother. Yet, she became the mother of Perez and contributed to the line of Christ. Joshua 6:22-25 shows how God used Rahab the harlot to help the men of Israel. Hebrews 11:25 and James 2:25 also mention Rahab. She was blessed as the mother of Boaz, the man who married Ruth—a godless woman from another culture. The book of Ruth reveals Boaz as an example of the redeemer that Christ would one day become.

Finally, Christ's lineage includes His mother Mary. Others considered this young woman a whore who was carrying a bastard child. And yet we know the truth. Even though Mary suffered this shame, she was a precious virgin chosen by God to give birth to the Lord Jesus Christ.

Second Corinthians 9:8 reminds, "And God is able to make all grace abound to you, so that in all things at all times, having all that you need, you will abound in every good work."

MEN OF GRACE

Historically, God has used men who have made terrible mistakes. Like the aforementioned women, these guys could have gotten stuck in the guilt and shame of their pasts, and God would never have been able to work through them in such mighty ways. It was only by God's grace and mercy that these men could get up and continue on.

For instance, when King David noticed Bathsheba bathing on a nearby rooftop, he lusted after her, committed adultery with her, and got her pregnant. Later, he had her husband murdered in order to conceal his sin. He struggled tremendously before God broke him and brought him to a place of repentance for his sin. Ultimately, God called David a man after His own heart.

Christ chose Peter to be one of His twelve disciples. Can you imagine walking with Christ in the flesh? Peter witnessed all of Christ's miracles and heard His messages firsthand. Then, at the Last Supper, Peter loudly declared that he would always be faithful to Jesus. Yet, after soldiers took Jesus the night before the crucifixion, Peter denied even knowing Him—not just once, but three times!

The story continues dramatically. Peter denied Christ out of human weakness. He feared being arrested and beaten, but later he wept bitterly over his denial. Furthermore, after the resurrection, Christ not only forgave Peter, He called him to establish the church. Before dying as a martyr, he asked his executioners to hang him upside down on the cross—a standard method of corporal punishment—because he was not worthy to be crucified like Christ. That's a big leap from the one who denied Christ to the one who gave his life for the cause of Christ. Clearly, God's grace had transformed Peter.

The great apostle Paul was originally named Saul—a man infamous for persecuting and killing Christians. Though he murdered many, God met him on the road to Damascus. There, he changed his name to Paul and changed his heart. In this way, Paul became the greatest New Testament evangelist.

His words in 1 Timothy 1:12-16 give me great hope: "I thank Christ Jesus our Lord, who has given me strength, that he considered me faithful, appointing me to his service. Even though I was once a blasphemer and a persecutor and a violent man, I was shown mercy because I acted in ignorance and unbelief. The grace of our Lord was poured out on me abundantly, along with the faith and love that are in Christ Jesus.

"Here is a trustworthy saying that deserves full acceptance: Christ Jesus came into the world to save sinners—of whom I am the worst. But for that very reason I was shown mercy so that in me, the worst of sinners, Christ Jesus might display his unlimited patience as an example for those who would believe on him and receive eternal life."

In 2 Corinthians 12:9-10, Paul also writes, "But He said to me, 'My grace is sufficient for you, for my power is made perfect in weakness.' Therefore, I will boast all the more gladly about my weaknesses, so that Christ's power may rest on me. That is why, for Christ sake, I delight in weaknesses, in insults, in hardships, in persecutions, in difficulties. For when I am weak, then I am strong."

God can graciously use flawed people! According to Paul, the deeper the sin, the greater the capacity for God's grace to abound. Have you noticed that Jesus hung out with the prostitutes and tax collectors? He sought out the people who needed Him the most—not those who had it all together.

Some people feel that if God forgives all of our sins, then we can do whatever we want and then ask forgiveness. But that's not the way it works. We must remember that God does not wink at sin. Disobedience grieves the heart of God. It is sin that sent Jesus to the cross. Grace is not cheap.

The Desire for Control

Sometimes, I desperately try to control the areas in my life as if they were expensive antique china. But keeping such a tight grasp on each one takes a lot of energy and attention. Furthermore, without God, those beautiful pieces of china become nothing more than fragile idols. If I trip along the path of life and drop these cherished possessions, they will fall to the floor and break into many pieces. At that point, I may scream for God to repair them.

"I won't repair those objects, but why don't you let me have the pieces?" God calmly says.

"No! If you won't fix it, I'll glue it back together myself," I angrily respond. "And if that doesn't work, I'll find someone else who can help." With that, I reach out to pick up the broken pieces of my life: pride, loneliness, fear, depression, and so on. But as I clutch the jagged pieces tightly, they make deep gashes in my hands.

"That looks very painful," God observes. "Why don't you let me have those now?" Part of me still wants to resist—to have control and to prove I can do this by myself. But, then I notice the blood dripping from my clenched hands, and realize that the pain is too great to continue in this way.

"God, I've made a really big mess with all these things I've held to so tightly," I finally concede. "Can you please help me?" As I open my hands and allow God to take the fragmented pieces that I have treasured for so long, I understand that only His hands can safely hold such sharp objects. Only His hands can make something broken into something new and beautiful.

THE BEAUTY OF BROKENNESS

For our tenth anniversary, my husband David and I spent a week in Charleston, South Carolina. While on vacation, I love browsing for antiques, and we found a shop that displayed the most breathtaking pieces I have ever seen! The most memorable piece was a wooden chest about three feet tall that was covered with broken pieces of Flow Blue china.

Flow Blue is a collector's dream because it is beautiful blue-and-white colored English china made during the 1800s. The makers of this chest had used broken pieces of china to create a masterpiece that gave me sticker shock. It cost $7,500, but I know that whoever purchases the piece will display it with great pride.

As I thought about that unique mosaic of broken china, I realized that God can do the very same thing with our lives. What may look like a pile of broken, ruined pieces is actually the raw materials for a beautiful masterpiece. God has a different perspective on what we feel should be swept up and thrown in the trash. The mistakes that we feel so ashamed of are still pieces He can use in His own signature pattern of grace.

Isn't the grace of God wonderful? We may deserve to be outcast and left in our shame, but God rescues us out of darkness and brings us into the radiance and purity of His light. Psalm 34:4-5 says, "I sought the LORD, and he answered me; he delivered me from all my fears. Those who look to him are radiant; their faces are never covered with shame."

Do You Need Grace?

So what are the issues you are dealing with? Are you like Jesse, the prodigal daughter who wandered far from home? Remember that you can be a prodigal without ever openly rebelling. Are you running away from the outstretched arms of your heavenly Father when you need to be running straight into them?

God is waiting for you to come home. He will run to meet you, forgive your shameful mistakes, and bring you back into loving fellowship with Him. Maybe, like me, you need time to learn life's lessons. Is God patiently trying to reteach you a lesson you forgot when you decided your way was better than His?

Are you hanging on to the pieces of your broken life, desperately hoping that you can somehow put them all back together? Have you realized that those broken areas are causing you only more pain and suffering? God is waiting for you to turn those over to Him. He is the only one who can make a masterpiece out of what you consider a mess.

twelve

BUILDING A HERITAGE: LEAVING A LEGACY OF GLORY

"For I know the plans I have for you,"
declares the LORD, "plans to prosper you
and not to harm you, plans to give you hope
and a future. Then you will call upon me,
and come and pray to me, and I will listen
to you. You will seek me and find me when
you seek me with all your heart."
JEREMIAH 29:11-13

few years ago, I watched Oprah Winfrey interview Reverend Billy Graham. I still remember her asking what had surprised him most about life. He said that he was amazed at the brevity of life. It had all passed by so quickly.

I agree with him. But when I was a kid, I thought time crawled. I felt like Christmas took five years to arrive. And I figured I would never turn thirteen. When that wonderful teenage birthday finally did show up, I was already dreaming of turning sixteen and getting my driver's license. College dragged on for quite some time, too—especially during exam weeks.

But after I finished school, time started to pick up speed. In fact, the older I get, the faster it goes. Now, November rolls around, and I think, "It can't be Thanksgiving again! We just did that a few months ago!" The only way I can get things to slow down is to stagger through another pregnancy, as I happen to be doing now. (Lately it seems each day lasts a week!)

However you perceive the pace of life, one thing's for sure: none of us know how much time we have left. For instance, on Saturday afternoons a group of men gets together to play basketball at our church's gymnasium. A few weeks ago, a thirty-three-year-old was playing ball there one minute, and in the next, he had fallen to the floor and died within the hour of a massive heart attack. He was a good athlete in great shape. How could he have known when he awoke that morning that it would somehow be the last day of his life?

I always think death happens to everybody else and, with this mindset, I never live like today might be my last. Instead, I meander through life, and I waste a lot of time. Sometimes, I realize that I've let an entire week slip by without serving Jesus or blessing anyone. Have you ever stopped to think what kind of legacy you will leave behind?

Unfortunately, after most funerals, only the family and close friends of the deceased remember them. This reality can make our lives seem very unimportant. Yet, God tells us that we can make a difference; that we can leave behind a legacy that makes an impact on future generations. My grandmother gave me a ring that I wear every day as a reminder of her. But she also prayed for me every day of my life, and I value that far more.

If, like Billy Graham, you view life as brief, what type of inheritance do you want to leave to others? When you are gone, what do you want people to say about you? Some may say that you had a great sense of humor or you were so sweet or that you made the best apple pie in the county.

I want people to remember me as someone who loved Jesus and others. They may also know that I struggled with my own heartaches and embraced God's grace. And I hope that is evident in the way I serve God. I want people to remember me as an authentic person, the what-you-see-is-what-you-get type.

Your Legacy

My friend Marge Caldwell—a woman you may have heard speak on Focus on the Family radio—is a precious believer, now in her 80s. She's slowed down, but she still works as a counselor at her church in Houston. She also continues traveling to speak and teach. She has mentored countless women through her godly example and through her stock encouragement: "Do not waste your valleys."

At one conference, I was scheduled to speak after she finished teaching. I felt inadequate to follow her, and started my speech by saying, "I don't know about you, but when I grow up, I want to be Marge Caldwell." Later, I realized that I wanted to emulate her because her life so clearly reflected the life of Christ.

As you ponder what kind of legacy you will leave, ask yourself these questions: "Am I leaving behind a legacy of perfection? Am I setting people up for failure because they feel that they will never be good enough? Will people remember my critical spirit more than anything else—that I never had a kind word to say about anyone?" Have you ever met a person with this kind of legacy?

Proverbs 3:5-6 says, "Trust in the LORD with all your heart and lean not on your own understanding; in all your ways acknowledge him, and he will make your paths straight." If we want to build a godly heritage, here are some areas in which we can grow.

BE A GIVER

The people who have affected me in the most positive ways are the ones who have been particularly generous with their time, love, acceptance, and encouragement. The giving of themselves has been a tremendous gift and blessing to my life! There are some gifts—both tangible and intangible—that will help you build a legacy of generosity. Think about those valuables and how to best share them with others.

BE AUTHENTIC

I appreciate *The Velveteen Rabbit* story because the rabbit discovers that being "real" doesn't require fancy gadgets or wind-up parts. For a toy to become real, it simply needs to be dearly loved by a child. I want to live in a way that other people know I am "real." I want to be approachable. I want to be honest enough about my own failures that people know they can safely share their own with me.

To be authentic, I need to admit that I don't have all the answers and that sometimes, I question God and His plan for my life. I don't want to play games with anyone or pretend I have it all together when I know no one else does either. I want to admit that I am in desperate need of the love, grace, and forgiveness of Christ.

I challenge you to be authentic so others can express their feelings without fearing your judgment. In other words, help people up when they fall—without criticizing them. Offer genuine love and support to those who are hurting.

BE A GOOD LISTENER

In our culture, we very often forget the importance of listening. We interrupt or simply stop listening when another person talks while we think of what we will say next. My friends and family know I like to talk, and some long ago dubbed me "The Mouth of the South." But we all need to give the gift of listening.

Some will stay in therapy for years just to have one hour a week when someone listens to them. It feels good to them to have undivided attention. Let's face it, attention feels great to all of us! But when is the last time you put your busyness on hold to focus on listening to your child, your spouse, or a close friend?

We need to have quality time where everything else is put on hold, where we sit face to face with good eye contact and open ears to find out how another person is really feeling. To invite this kind of conversation, you might ask, "What is happening in your life? How are you really doing? What are your concerns? How can I be praying for you specifically? Is there anything you need from me right now?" Showing genuine concern and listening carefully communicates that you value that person.

When I struggle, I don't necessarily want someone to try and fix the problem for me. Instead, I want her to hug me. I want that person to say that she knows I'm hurting, and she cares. Within the body of Christ, the church, we are called to this ministry of listening. Yet, how many pat their dog more than they hug their children and others?

BE A FORGIVER
No one ever says, "When I grow up, I want to be a bitter old woman." Yet, that's exactly where we're headed if we refuse to offer forgiveness to others. Do you struggle in this area? For starters, confess to God that you want to grow. Without change, you will pass bitterness to your children.

Realize that women who won't forgive typically suffer from unresolved anger. They often also feel isolated, abandoned, depressed, or caught in a cycle of compulsive perfectionism. But God teaches forgiveness and models it through Jesus. We are called to love and forgive, just as God loves and forgives us!

We also need to know when to ask for forgiveness. Some of the most healing words in a damaged relationship include, "I was wrong. I am sorry. Will you please forgive me? I love you."

BE AN IMITATOR OF GOD
During my second pregnancy, I was involved in a serious car accident. Thankfully, my unborn son Christian was not harmed,

but I suffered a painful back injury. And as my pregnancy weight increased, my back pain increased. To give those aching muscles extra support, I would often stand with my hands on my hips.

While visiting my parents, my father laughed when he noticed my two-year-old daughter Elisabeth standing in the same way. She was not consciously doing this, but because she was always with me, loves me, and wants to be just like me, she was imitating my actions. When I realized how well she could copy me, I got a new-found appreciation for Ephesians 5:1, which says, "Be imitators of God, therefore, as dearly loved children."

This verse confirms that God dearly loves us because we are His little children. And in the same way that Elisabeth wants to emulate me because she loves me, when we love God, we want to be like Him. We want to act like He acts, look like He looks, and do the things that He does. But it takes spending time together to do that.

How much time do you spend with God? When we spend time in God's Word, when we pray and listen to God, when we fellowship and share our journey with other believers, we will begin to imitate His loving character more and more.

Galatians 5:22-23 explains that this process yields the fruit of the Spirit: love, joy, peace, patience, gentleness, goodness, and hope. By imitating Christ, you will gradually notice your sense of abandonment being replaced with God's unconditional love and acceptance. Joy and light will move into where the darkness of depression used to reign. Peace will overshadow fear, and patience will soothe the person whose temper used to snap at small annoyances. A gentle spirit will cover the anxiety that once seemed constant. Goodness and kindness instead of harsh judgments will overflow from your soul. Finally, hope in Christ will replace despair.

BE A PERSON OF PRAYER

Often, when children are young, we say a bedtime prayer with them. But as they get older, they grow out of that bedtime ritual.

Yet, to establish a legacy of prayer, children need to hear us pray regularly and specifically. If the only prayer your children hear is the blessing at the dinner table, try gathering the family for a regular devotional time that includes prayers where everyone can freely share their requests.

You may not know how to pray in front of others. That's okay. If you know how to talk, you know how to pray. Just talk to God. Tell Him how wonderful He is, and thank Him for providing again for your family. You can also pray for specific needs and for people outside of your family. Then, rejoice together when God answers your prayers. Some keep a family prayer journal and write down the answers as a reminder of God's faithfulness. Establishing a consistent prayer time shows children that you communicate with God all the time—not just during crisis situations.

BE A DREAM BUILDER

Psalm 78:4-8 says, "We will not hide them from their children; we will tell the next generation the praiseworthy deeds of the LORD, his power, and the wonders he has done. He decreed statutes for Jacob and established the law in Israel, which he commanded our forefathers to teach their children, so the next generation would know them, even the children yet to be born, and they in turn would tell their children. Then they would put their trust in God and would not forget his deeds but would keep his commands. They would not be like their forefathers—a stubborn and rebellious generation, whose hearts were not loyal to God."

We need to pray for God's vision for our children because it can be very tempting to want to impose our vision on them, especially if we have unfinished business from our own childhood. Sometimes, we are not even aware of that motivation. We merely tell ourselves, "I want what is best for my children. I only want them to have the things I was not able to have, or to do the things I could not do."

We need to ask ourselves if we're living vicariously through our children. If so, it's time to set our agenda aside and pursue God's plan for our children. At that point, we are on a healthy track to becoming "dream builders." As a dream builder, you need to encourage your children in the things they seek to accomplish—even if you consider those goals unrealistic.

For instance, if your daughter is 5'5" and dreams of playing basketball, don't tell her she'll never make it because she's too short. Instead, tell her to practice as much as possible, play basketball with good players who will teach her, and give it all she's got! If the dream fails, she'll come back to you for support because you were a cheerleader all along. But if the dream fails and you were critical from the start, the child or teen will pull further away from you in order to avoid the pain of hearing, "I told you so."

Also, ask your children and teens about what they want to be when they grow up. Sometimes they have no idea, and other times the answer will change. If they have an idea, and you know someone who is in that chosen profession, set up a lunch date with that person so your teen can ask questions and learn which steps that individual took to attain his or her dreams. Notice their interests and work to cultivate those interests.

So much of our time with children and teens is spent telling them what they haven't done right (for example, "When are you ever going to remember to take out the trash? You're room looks like a tornado hit it! I can't believe you got another 'C' in algebra!"). Lest we forget, the teen years are difficult. Hormones rage, acne appears, and many feel insecure and uncertain about their future. No one could pay me enough to relive those years!

Teens desperately need encouragement. They need to know that we believe in them and in their dreams! Hebrews 10:24 says, "Let us consider how we can spur one another on toward love and good deeds."

I remember when my former pastor, Dr. Hall Habecker, shared this anecdote at Dallas Bible Church: "When the great artist Benjamin West was a young boy, he decided to paint a picture of his sister while his mother was not at home. He got out the bottles of ink and started, but soon had an awful mess. When his mother returned, she saw the mess, but instead of scolding him, she picked up the portrait and declared, 'What a beautiful picture of your sister!' Then she kissed him. Later in life, he said, 'With that kiss, I became a painter.'"[1]

In 1849, Nathaniel Hawthorne was dismissed from his government job at a customhouse. He went home in despair that day. However, after his wife listened to his tale of woe, she set a pen and inkwell on the table, lit the fire, put her arms around his shoulders and said, "Now you will be able to write your novel." Hawthorne did, and the literary world gained a classic—*The Scarlet Letter.*

When I was fifteen years old, I felt God calling me into the ministry as a Christian counselor. Many people in my church discouraged me. They said that psychology and theology could not be joined together. My mother, on the other hand, never questioned my desire. Instead, she encouraged me to follow the path that God had called me to. I also dreamed about writing, but I had no idea how God would ever work that out.

I used to call these desires "my little Jesus dreams" because I knew they were from God. After all, the Lord plants seed of promise in the soil of our hearts. I did things to delay their growth at times by following the wrong path of disobedience. But God did not let those seeds rot. That was another expression of God's grace to me. Eventually, in His faithfulness, He drew me back to Him and those seeds began to grow and take root as He brought those dreams to fruition.

If I asked you to remember the most damaging thing anyone ever said to you, it would instantly come to mind. Words are so powerful to do damage, but they can also be used to give confidence and hope to another person. So, we have the power to speak words that hurt or words that heal. We can either build up or tear down. God calls us to encourage our children to love

Him and serve Him in whatever dream they pursue. I want to have a legacy as the loudest cheerleader my children ever had!

BE A RECONCILER

If you've passed on a damaging inheritance and your children have already flown the coop, be not dismayed. You're not alone. Many parents realize their mistakes long after they make them. Furthermore, admitting your mistakes and taking responsibility for them takes a lot of maturity and represents a healthy step in the right direction. Just think of all the people who never do either one.

Instead of letting guilt overwhelm and paralyze you, you must turn the past over to God. Not only does He desire to be the Lord of our present and future, He wants to be the Lord of the past. And His grace can redeem your past. Jesus died to pay for your past.

Romans 8:1 says, "There is no condemnation for those who are in Christ Jesus." Claim that promise! Don't allow Satan to sell you on the lie that you will always be guilty and ashamed. Once you ask for God's forgiveness and have begun forgiving yourself, you need to seek reconciliation with those you've hurt.

In chapter 6 I shared the story of Ann—the abused woman who had grown children by the time she sought help. After some time in therapy, she realized how much she had damaged her own children by repeating some of the family anger. For years she struggled with deep grief and guilt. Ultimately, she realized that only the Holy Spirit could give her forgiveness and peace.

An important part of her healing process involved accepting that she could not change the past, but that she could work to break the chain of family secrets and denial. To accomplish this, she met individually with her now adult children and admitted the specifics of how she knew she had hurt them. She then explained what she had been learning and asked them to forgive her. She even brought one daughter along to a therapy session and allowed her to share safely how she felt toward Ann. Ann even offered to pay for therapy if her children wanted to work through their issues.

Today, her children respect her for being honest and for at long last taking responsibility for her actions as their mother. It is never too late to say, "I was wrong. I am sorry. How can I make amends? Please forgive me."

New Beginnings

Recently I gave birth to our daughter Mary Camille. I will admit that although I love my children dearly, I am one of those women who *hate* being pregnant. I feel nauseated for months, my back hurts, I can't sleep, I can't breathe, my hands and feet swell, even my nose gets fat. . . . You get the picture. The thing that keeps me going during pregnancy is thinking about the literal fruit of my labor. Envisioning a tiny new life coming into our family encourages me to hang in there.

Now as I look into the face of our child, she seems so hopeful, so innocent—with a life full of promise for the future. When she smiles, I sometimes find myself expecting her to gain a little voice and cry out with laughter, "Look at me growing! I'm finally here!" I often hear people say that they wish they could just go back and start life over. God offers us each the chance to start out fresh and clean through His forgiveness and grace.

Some of the choices we've made can never be erased. But babies encourage me to remember that *God is the God of second chances*. Even in the darkest seasons of our lives, when everything inside us feels used up and dead, He patiently waits to clean us up and allows us to start over again.

Even if you believe you've wasted your life, He continues to consider you with compassion. In fact, He knows how to help each of us live healthy and fruitful lives that will bring honor and glory to Him as we give Him credit for our new beginning. We are humbled and grateful because we know that on our own we could never start over. But by His wonderful grace, God gives us another opportunity.

Finishing Well

Hebrews 12:1-3 says, "Therefore, since we are surrounded by such a great cloud of witnesses, let us throw off everything that hinders and the sin that so easily entangles, and let us run the race marked out for us. Let us fix our eyes on Jesus, the author and perfecter of our faith, who for the joy set before him endured the cross, scorning its shame and sat down at the right hand of the throne of God. Consider him who endured such opposition from sinful men, so that you will not grow weary and lose heart."

When you watch Olympic runners perform, how many carry a suitcase or television as they race around the track? As a matter of fact, they now strip down to the most scant clothing to be as light and streamlined as possible. These verses tell us to do the same thing, to put aside anything—sin, relationships, addictions, idols, and so on—that burdens us as we run our spiritual race.

As in all races, the way you finish is always more important than the way you start. Runners keep their eyes on the finish line. They don't scope the crowd or turn to see who's running behind them. We are told to keep our eyes on Jesus who has gone ahead and already triumphantly crossed the finish line. Along the way, He endured the pain of the cross, and He despised the sin and shame that was put on Him there.

You too can despise the shame that sin has brought into your life. But Christ is our example. He didn't get stuck by loathing the sin and shame forever. Instead, He focused on the finish line and saw the joy of our salvation and the joy of being reunited in heaven with God.

Christ's finished work gives us the hope and the strength we need to break the cycle of generational sin and shame. In this way, we can leave an inheritance of truthful beliefs, spiritual blessings, and emotionally healthy dynamics for our children, our spouse, our friends, and following generations.

Psalm 119:111-112 says, "Your statutes are my heritage forever; they are the joy of my heart. My heart is set on keeping your decrees to the very end."

Find encouragement and "hope for your heart." Through the redeeming love and healing grace of God, every person can break free from shame and live a life of freedom that brings glory and honor to God!

Bible Study

WEEK ONE

1. What do you think a shameless Garden of Eden was like for Adam and Eve? Try to describe what their relationship with God was like.

2. When sin entered the world through Adam and Eve's disobedience, what happened to their relationship with God? How did it change? Read Job 31:33, Isaiah 47:3, and Romans 3:23.

3. The moment Adam and Eve sinned, a plan of redemption was set in motion. Why was this necessary? Read Romans 5:12-21 and 6:23.

4. Choice is the first thing God gave human beings. Describe how the choices you've made have affected your life. Read Deuteronomy 30:19-20 and Joshua 24:15.

5. What are some examples of external sin in your life? What are some examples of internal or hidden sins in your life? Read 1 Corinthians 6:9-19, Galatians 5:19-21, and Ephesians 2:3.

6. What comes to mind when you hear the word *shame?* Read Genesis 3:7,10 and Romans 8:15.

7. Shame is described in chapter 1 as either toxic and life-destroying or nourishing and healthy. Give examples of each and consider how shame affects your life for the worse and for the better. Read John 3:19-21 and 16:8.

8. Think about the differences between the true and false self. How do you see the two in your life? Read Proverbs 23:7 and John 16:8.

9. Both true and false guilt can be a red flag for sin. Where does false guilt come from? Read Acts 2:37, 1 Corinthians 4:3-4, and 1 Timothy 4:1-2.

10. How can a personal relationship with Jesus Christ heal the negative effects of shame? Read John 8:32 and Ephesians 4:22-24.

11. What would your life be like if you experienced emotional wholeness? Read Psalm 23:3 and Job 33:25-26.

12. Who is the only One who can give you your heart's desire? Read Psalm 21:2, 37:3-5, and 145:19.

13. Do you think there is ever a time when God will stop searching for His wayward children? Read Psalm 139:23, Jeremiah 17:10, and Romans 8:27.

WEEK TWO

1. What is a family legacy?

2. When a family heirloom is passed from one generation to the next, what does this gift say? Read Genesis 24:53 and 37:3-4.

3. Not every person receives a tangible inheritance, but *everyone* receives an intangible emotional inheritance. Describe the emotional inheritance in your family. Is it positive or negative? Read Deuteronomy 5:9-10, Isaiah 54:13, and Jeremiah 32:17-18.

4. How would you define a "dysfunctional family"?

5. What did you once consider normal family behavior that you now see as unhealthy? Read Proverbs 22:6, Proverbs 22:24-45, and Ephesians 4:17-24.

6. What are some common unspoken rules in shaming, dysfunctional families? Which rules apply to your family?

7. What were the generational sins that Abraham and Sarah passed on in their family? Read Genesis 21:10 and 26:11-13.

8. How did Isaac and Jacob follow in their parents' footsteps? Read Genesis 26:7-11, 27:18-24, and 37:3.

9. How did Joseph break the chain of generational sin? Read Genesis 50:15-21 and Ephesians 4:32.

10. What were your ideas about God during your childhood? How has this affected your view of God as an adult? Read Psalm 127:3-5 and Ephesians 6:4.

11. How does God's truth set you free from the bondage of generational sin? Read Psalm 71:5-6 and 1 John 3:19-22.

WEEK THREE

1. Pigpen had a cloud of dirt and dust that followed him wherever he went. Name some of the clouds of shame that you have experienced in your own life.

2. Why do the clouds of shame due to abuse produce a sense of isolation and rejection? Read Isaiah 59:12-15.

3. Why is the shame of abuse *always* about the perpetrator and *never* about the victim? Read Ephesians 6:4 and Colossians 3:21.

4. In the author's opinion, what type of abuse is the most damaging and shaming of all? Why? Read 2 Samuel 13:1-29 and 1 Corinthians 6:9-10.

5. Passive abuse is not as obvious as active abuse. Why is abandonment a passive form of abuse?

6. List reasons why significance, worth, and affirmation are so important to the development of a child.

7. When the role of parent and child are reversed, how does it affect the child?

8. Chapter 1 briefly describes the true and false self. Which characteristics of the true and false self do you see in your own life? Were any of these new insights for you?

9. Who keeps you in bondage through false thinking? Read Ephesians 2:2 and 6:12.

10. Jesus said, "I am the way, the truth and the life." How does He help you see your true self? Read Psalm 51:6 and Ephesians 4:15.

11. How has God lovingly planned to deliver you from your painful past and given you hope for your wounded heart? Read Romans 6:21-23 and 2 Thessalonians 2:16-17.

WEEK FOUR

1. Why are outward appearances so important in our churches today? Read 1 Samuel 16:7 and Luke 16:15.

2. What would be the truthful interpretation of "Praise the Lord anyhow"?

3. Why do you think so many in churches try to keep up a good front and "fake it for the brethren"? Read Matthew 6:1.

4. What did Jesus mean when He described the Pharisees as, "Whitewashed tombs full of dead man's bones?" Read Matthew 23:27-28.

5. What keeps Christians from admitting their weaknesses and needs to others?

6. When tragedy strikes, why do some Christians expect the hurting person to respond with peace and joy?

7. If doubt and heartache are shared in confidence, what is the needed response? Read Psalm 147:3 and Isaiah 61:1.

8. Why are wounds from the body of Christ more painful than wounds from the world? Read Proverbs 18:19.

9. List some of the legalistic rules you have experienced in the church. Read Isaiah 29:13 and Colossians 2:20-23.

10. Discuss the pride and insecurity of a person who has a critical spirit. Read Galatians 5:15.

11. How can you be a place of safety and acceptance for others? Are you? Read Romans 15:1 and Ephesians 4:32.

12. Who is hurt when cliques form at church? Has this ever happened to you?

13. Many have experienced shame, hurt, and rejection in church settings. What does God give us in exchange for these wounds? Read Isaiah 54:10 and 1 Corinthians 2:9.

WEEK FIVE

1. List the ways that you identify with Wendy.

2. Proverbs 23:7 teaches that whatever you say to yourself has a definite impact on how you feel about yourself. What needs to change about your self-talk?

3. What do perfectionistic people believe about themselves?

4. Why do all imperfect human beings need a relationship with a loving, perfect Savior? Read Mark 2:17, Romans 3:23, and Romans 5:8.

5. Discuss codependency and some of its common traits. Which traits do you recognize in your life?

6. How can your unawareness of root issues contribute to the various addictions you experience?

7. In Romans 7:15-20, Paul explains that he does things that he really doesn't want to do. List some addictive behaviors.

8. How can addictions be multi-generational?

9. A healthy understanding of the truth of God's love is essential to stopping addictive behaviors. What does God say about you? Read Romans 8:35-39, 1 Corinthians 6:19-20, and Philippians 4:13.

10. How are idolatry and addictions related? Read 1 John 2:15-17 and Colossians 3:1-4.

11. Read Isaiah 61:1-3. These verses give a wonderful description of beauty for ashes. What does this mean in your life?

12. God waits for you to come to Him. How does He communicate that to you? Read Romans 5:19-21 and 1 Timothy 1:14-16.

WEEK SIX

1. What were Ann's reasons for carrying her deep anger?

2. Incest and sexual abuse damage victims to the core. What is the root cause of this damage? Read Psalm 51:3, John 15:22, and Romans 5:12.

3. Why do sexual abuse victims experience confusion when they consider their experience?

4. Sexual abuse is described as a "splinter driven deeply into a victim's heart." In what areas have you experienced splinters of pain?

5. Women who have been sexually abused often blame themselves. How does this keep them from recovering?

6. How does the enemy, Satan, use the shame of abuse to twist your God-given need to be loved? Read 1 Peter 5:8.

7. Roots of bitterness will overwhelm a victim if she refuses to forgive the perpetrator(s) of the abuse. Read Romans 12:14-21, Ephesians 4:31-32, and 1 Peter 3:8-9.

8. Who gives you the ability and strength to forgive? Read Matthew 6:9,12, Acts 13:38-41, and Colossians 1:13-14.

9. Forgiveness is a process. What is the first step?

10. God is in the business of taking your shame-filled past and turning it into something valuable that He can use in the lives of others. Won't you let Him do that for you today? Read Psalm 30:11-12 and 2 Corinthians 1:3-7.

WEEK SEVEN

1. Many women who have aborted a baby deny their feelings about this event to avoid the pain. What are the ways you have used denial as a means of protection?

2. If you have had an abortion, have you ever told your story? Use separate paper or a journal to tell God—and yourself—what really happened. Healing can only begin when you face the truth.

3. List any Post Abortion Syndrome (PAS) symptoms you have experienced.

4. Anger grows roots of deep bitterness. Ask God to reveal the sources of your anger. Then write "safe" letters—letters not meant to be mailed—in order to express your anger.

5. If you need to forgive yourself, what steps can you take to pursue forgiveness?

6. Releasing anger is a process. Spend some time in prayer. Have hope; the healing will come with time.

7. Whom do you need to forgive?

8. Read 2 Samuel 12:15-23. When David's infant son died, David said, "I will go to him, but he will not return to me." What did he mean?

9. How do the verses in chapter 7 encourage women who've aborted that they will one day see their child in heaven?

WEEK EIGHT

1. What is the world's view of the "perfect woman"? How does that view affect the way you feel about yourself?

2. In what areas are you most content with your body?

3. In what areas are you most discontent with how you look? What are three things you would change about your body?

4. What is your current view of God? Do you see Him as a critical judge? Do you view Him as a friend? Do you feel that He loves you?

5. What has shaped your view of God?

6. When women stuff their food, what else are they stuffing?

7. Do you ever use food to keep your painful emotions at bay? If so, when are you most likely to use food?

8. How do the truths of Romans 12:1-2 apply to someone who suffers from an eating disorder?

9. How are you affected by the "garbage in, garbage out" philosophy? How does God desire to change your negative and shaming thinking?

10. What have you done in order to try to be perfect? How do you treat yourself when you make a mistake? How has perfectionism affected your relationships with others?

11. How would learning to love and accept yourself just the way you are change your life?

WEEK NINE

1. Why do good marriages take so much hard work?

2. Marriage helps point out areas where you and your spouse may need to change. Why is this so difficult for most to accept?

3. Why does divorce represent a quick fix for so many?

4. How are children affected by divorce? If your parents divorced, how did that affect you? Read 2 Corinthians 1:3-4. How do these verses encourage you? How do they comfort you? Finally, how do they give you hope and direction for future ministry opportunities?

5. Why do people seek a mate who is an emotional equal?

6. How can you accept divorced women and men?

7. Explain why "holding onto resentment as if it were a treasure of great worth" is a foolish idea.

8. Building emotional walls of protection can keep you from having an intimate relationship with God. Why?

9. Read John 4:4-42. Jesus told the woman at the well that she had been married not once, not twice, but five times. He added that the man she was living with was not her husband. In that culture, only a man could initiate divorce. After five divorces, she must have suffered a great deal of rejection and pain. But how did Jesus treat this woman? How does His tenderness and forgiveness encourage your heart? If Jesus could talk with you about your past, what do you think He would say to you?

10. Why is forgiveness an essential ingredient to finding encouragement and healing after a divorce?

11. How does the great "I AM" deliver you from your fears and turn your sorrow into joy? Read Psalm 30:11-12.

Week Ten

1. Describe the "perfect woman" image the media projects.

2. How can the truths of Scripture radically affect our sense of worth? Read John 8:31 and Romans 8:2.

3. Since the fall of Adam and Eve, we have all struggled with emptiness and feelings of insignificance. Who is the only One who can fulfill your deepest needs? Read 2 Corinthians 5:17 and Ephesians 2:4-5.

4. Describe how believing the 20/60/20 truth would change the way you value the acceptance of others.

5. Read Matthew 10:29-31. What do these verses mean to you?

6. God will *never* forget us and will love us forever. How does that truth comfort you? Read Isaiah 49:15-16, Jeremiah 31:3, and Hebrews 7:25.

7. How would you respond if someone asked, "Who are you?" What does your answer say about your relationship with God?

8. How does the truth that you are loved and accepted by God set you free? Read Proverbs 8:17, Romans 8:35-39, and Titus 3:4-7.

9. What does this statement mean to you, "You know so much about God in your head, and so little about Him in your heart"?

10. Meditate on one of God's greatest attributes—His love. Read John 15:13, Romans 5:8, and Ephesians 5:2.

11. What is God's gift to you? Read John 4:10, Romans 6:23, and James 1:17.

12. Sin is solvable. What a relief! What do Psalm 103:10-12, 1 John 1:9, and 1 John 4:4 mean to you personally?

13. When God's Word confirms that you are a woman of *great* value, how does that make you feel?

WEEK ELEVEN

1. Were you ever a prodigal daughter in your relationship with your parents or God? Explain.

2. What does the amazing grace of God mean to you? How have you seen God's grace in your own life?

3. Read Psalm 103:10-14. How do these truths affect your life today?

4. God did all the restoration work by sending Jesus as the perfect lamb. Read Ephesians 2:8-10, 2 Timothy 1:9, and 1 Peter 1:18-19, and write what they mean to you.

5. Why do we need to learn the same lessons time and time again?

6. "It's not wrong to be weak. It really is okay!" Do you agree or disagree with this statement? Why? Read 2 Corinthians 12:9-10 and 13:4.

7. Read Hebrews 13:5,8. What do these verses mean to you?

8. God's women of grace were all weak and sinful. What did God do in their lives?

9. Scripture is full of examples of men who were given second chances. Discuss some of these men listed under the heading "Men of Grace." How did God redeem their lives?

10. What does God really want when He says, "Let go, and give me all the pieces of your life." Read Romans 12:1-2 and Galatians 2:20.

11. What is the beauty of brokenness? Read Psalm 34:17-19, Psalm 51:17, Isaiah 57:1, and Isaiah 66:2.

12. God is the only One who can make a masterpiece out of our biggest messes in life. Will you allow Him to do that for you today?

Week Twelve

1. Billy Graham has stated that he is amazed at the brevity of life. What does God say about this subject? Read Job 14:1-2, Psalm 39:5, Psalm 90:10, and James 4:14.

2. What kind of legacy do you think you have? What do you want people to say about you after your death?

3. Think about the phrase, "Don't waste your valleys." Describe what that means to you.

4. How do you become conformed to the image of Christ? Read 1 Corinthians 15:49, Philippians 3:20-21, and Colossians 3:9-10.

5. List some ways that you can give the gift of "authenticity" to others.

6. How can you be a better listener? Read Proverbs 10:19, Ecclesiastes 5:1-2, and James 1:19.

7. Christ is the ultimate example of how to forgive. How can you learn to forgive? Read Matthew 18:21-22, Ephesians 4:32, Romans 12:14-21, and 1 Peter 3:8-9.

8. When you love God, you want to obey Him and be like Him. How do you imitate Jesus? Read Ephesians 5:1, Philippians 3:17, 4:9, and 1 Thessalonians 1:6.

9. How can prayer be a gift you give to others? Read 2 Corinthians 1:11, Colossians 4:12, and Hebrews 4:16.

10. How can you support your children's dreams? In what ways can you encourage the dreams of your spouse and friends?

11. God is the God of second chances. In what areas has He given you second chances?

12. Read 1 Corinthians 9:24, 2 Timothy 4:7, and Hebrews 12:1-3. Runners fix their eyes on the finish line. How do Christians finish the race of life well?

Bibliography

Dan Allender, *The Wounded Heart*, Colorado Springs, CO: NavPress, 1990.

Stephen Arterburn and Jack Felton, *Toxic Faith*, Nashville: Thomas Nelson: Oliver Nelson, 1991.

Gary Bergel, with C. Everett Koop, M.D., *When You Were Formed in Secret*, Reston, VA: Intercessors for America, 1986.

John Bradshaw, *Healing the Shame That Binds You*, Deerfield Beach, FL: Health Communications, Inc., 1988.

Dave Carder, Earl Henslin, John Townsend, Henry Cloud, Alice Brawand, *Secrets of Your Family Tree*, Chicago, IL: Moody, 1991.

Richard Paul Evans, *The Locket*, New York: Pocket Books, 1998.

Robert Hemfelt, Frank Minirth, and Paul Meier, *Love Is a Choice*, Nashville: Thomas Nelson, 1989.

Robert Hemfelt and Paul Warren, *Kids Who Carry Our Pain*, Nashville: Thomas Nelson, 1990.

C. S. Lewis, *The Four Loves*, New York: Harcourt Brace Jovanovich, Inc., 1960.

Max Lucado, *The Gift to All People,* Sisters, OR: Multnomah, 1999.

Gerald G. May, *Addiction and Grace*, San Francisco, CA: Harper, 1988.

Robert McGee, *The Search for Significance*, Houston, TX: Rapha, 1987.

Frank Minirth, Paul Meier, Robert Hemfelt and Sharon Sneed, *Love Hunger: Recovery from Food Addiction,* Nashville: Thomas Nelson: Oliver-Nelson Books, 1990.

Gary Moon, *Homesick for Eden*, Ann Arbor, Michigan: Servant Publications, 1997.

Ken Parker, *Reclaiming Your Inner Child*, Nashville: Thomas Nelson, 1993.

Suzanne Schlosberg, "Questions and Answers," *Shape Magazine*, August 2000.

David Seamands, *Healing of Memories*, New York: Inspirational Press, 1985.

David Seamands, "Perfectionism: Fraught with Fruits of Self-Destruction," *Christianity Today*, April 10, 1981.

Lewis Smedes, *Shame and Grace*, San Francisco: HarperCollins, 1993.

Malcolm Smith, *Forgiveness*, Tulsa, OK: Pillar, 1992.

Dr. Henry Townsend, *Changes That Heal*, Grand Rapids, MI: Zondervan Publishing House, 1992.

Jeanette Vought, *Post-Abortion Trauma: 9 Steps to Recovery*, Grand Rapids, MI: Zondervan, 1991.

Pam Vredevelt, Deborah Newman, Harry Beverly, and Frank Minirth, *The Thin Disguise*, Nashville: Thomas Nelson, 1992.

Sandra Wilson, *Released from Shame*, Downers Grove, IL: InterVarsity Press, 1990.

Philip Yancey, *What's So Amazing About Grace*, Grand Rapids, MI: Zondervan, 1997.

Notes

CHAPTER 2
1. Dr. Robert Hemfelt, Dr. Frank Minirth, Dr. Paul Meier, *Love Is a Choice* (Nashville: Thomas Nelson, 1989), p. 65.
2. Robert Hemfelt and Paul Warren, *Kids Who Carry Our Pain* (Nashville: Thomas Nelson, 1990), p. 23.

CHAPTER 3
1. Dr. Robert Hemfelt, Dr. Frank Minirth, and Dr. Paul Meier, *Love Is a Choice* (Nashville, TN: Thomas Nelson, 1989), p. 54.
2. Dr. Henry Townsend, *Changes That Heal* (Grand Rapids, MI: Zondervan Publishing House, 1992), p. 92.
3. Gershen Kaufman, as quoted by John Bradshaw in *Healing the Shame That Binds You*, (Deerfield Beech, FL: Health Communications, 1988), p. 8.
4. Lane Ogden quoted from a seminar delivered at the Minirth-Meier Clinic, Richardson, TX, November 1989.

CHAPTER 4
1. Dr. David Ferguson and Dr. Don McMinn, *Top 10 Intimacy Needs* (Austin, TX: Intimacy Press, 1994), pp. 11-12.
2. Stephen Arterburn and Jack Felton, *Toxic Faith* (Nashville, TN: Oliver Nelson, 1991), p. 54.
3. Chuck Swindoll, in the foreword to Dave Carder, Earl Henslin, John Townsend, Henry Cloud, and Alice Brawand, *Secrets of Your Family Tree* (Chicago, IL: Moody, 1991), pp. 9-10.

CHAPTER 5
1. David Burns, "The Perfectionist's Script for Self-Defeat," *Psychology Today*, Nov. 1980, p. 34.
2. Stephen Arterburn and Jack Felton, *Toxic Faith* (Nashville, TN: Oliver Nelson, 1991), p. 104.

CHAPTER 6
1. David Seamands, *Healing of Memories* (New York: Inspirational Press, 1985), p. 360.
2. Dan Allender, *The Wounded Heart* (Colorado Springs, CO: NavPress, 1990), p. 49.

3. Philip Yancey, *What's So Amazing About Grace* (Grand Rapids, MI: Zondervan, 1997), pp. 98-99.
4. Lewis Smedes, *Shame and Grace* (San Francisco: Harper-Collins, 1993), pp. 136,141.

CHAPTER 7
1. Jeanette Vought, *Post-Abortion Trauma: 9 Steps to Recovery,* (Grand Rapids, MI: Zondervan, 1991), p. 47.
2. Gary Bergel, with C. Everett Koop, M.D., *When You Were Formed in Secret,* (Reston, VA: Intercessors for America, 1986), pp. 1-6.

CHAPTER 8
1. Pam Vredevelt, Deborah Newman, Harry Beverly, and Frank Minirth, *The Thin Disguise* (Nashville, TN: Thomas Nelson, 1992), p. 83.
2. Frank Minirth, Paul Meier, Robert Hemfelt, and Sharon Sneed, *Love Hunger: Recovery from Food Addiction* (Nashville, TN: Oliver-Nelson Books, 1990), pp. 29-30.
3. Suzanne Schlosberg, "Questions and Answers," *Shape Magazine,* August, 2000, p. 94.

CHAPTER 9
1. Ken Parker, *Reclaiming Your Inner Child* (Nashville, TN: Thomas Nelson, 1993), p. 83.
2. Robert McGee, *The Search for Significance* (Houston, TX: Rapha, 1987), p. 26.
3. Malcolm Smith, *Forgiveness* (Tulsa, OK: Pillar, 1992), pp. 6-7.
4. Richard Paul Evans, *The Locket* (New York: Pocket Books, 1998), p. 202.
5. C. S. Lewis, *The Four Loves* (New York: Harcourt Brace Jovanovich, Inc., 1960), p. 169.

CHAPTER 10
1. Robert McGee, *The Search for Significance* (Houston, TX: Rapha, 1987), p. 5.

CHAPTER 12
1. Dr. Hall Habecker, quoted from a message delivered at Dallas Bible Church, Dallas, December 1996.

About the Author

Cynthia Spell Humbert was a therapist with the Minirth-Meier Clinic in Dallas, for seven years, and a frequent guest speaker on the Clinic's national radio program. She has earned master's degrees in Counseling Psychology and Christian Counseling. Her clinical experience includes group, marriage, family, and individual therapy. She has specialized in counseling women and has a desire for teaching them the truth about their incredible value to God!

Cynthia is vulnerably real, exposing the frailty in her own life to create a bridge for her audience between pain and godly potential. Above all else, she is a woman who loves the Lord and recognizes His sovereignty and grace as being the single answer to our deepest cry. She testifies passionately to Christ's sacrificial and unconditional love in our lives regardless of who we are or what we've done.

Cynthia combines the healing truths of Scripture with sound psychological principles. Her credentials and experience as a Christian therapist, nationally popular speaker, and author have made her a compelling and effective witness, but it is her heart that will reach you. And it is her message that will convict and convince you that it is from a broken heart that God shapes the pieces of a masterpiece.

She and her husband David live in Austin, Texas with their three young children: Elisabeth, Christian, and Mary Camille.

For information on scheduling Cynthia to speak, contact her at: 1250 Capital of Texas Highway South, Bldg. 3, Suite 400, Austin, TX 78746. Fax: 512-306-0761; e-mail humbert@viafamily.com.

Please contact Cynthia by e-mail or at the above address to comment on this book or to send in your own story of God's healing grace.

ADDITIONAL BOOKS IN THE WISDOM FOR WOMEN SERIES.

Calm My Anxious Heart

Filled with encouragement and a twelve-week Bible study for overcoming anxiety, *Calm My Anxious Heart* will help you experience the calm and contentment promised in Scripture.

Calm My Anxious Heart (Linda Dillow) $14
Calm My Anxious Heart: My Mercies Journal (Linda Dillow) $10

Becoming a Woman of Influence

See how your struggles and triumphs can inspire others. Carol Kent helps you prepare to become a valued mentor who leaves an eternal mark.

Becoming a Woman of Influence (Carol Kent) $14

Through His Eyes

This book replaces the pressures women face with messages straight from Scripture. Perfect for women frustrated with not living up to worldly expectations.

Through His Eyes (Kathy Collard Miller) $13

Holy Habits

By examining the character of God, you will learn how to live each day intentionally and see your life the same way God does. Includes a ten-week Bible study.

Holy Habits (Mimi Wilson) $11

Under the Circumstances

With a blend of Scripture and personal anecdotes, Judy Hampton demonstrates how changing your perspective from human to godly allows you to gain from the challenges life throws your way.

Under the Circumstances (Judy Hampton) $11

Get your copies today at your local bookstore, visit our website at www.navpress.com, or call (800) 366-7788 and ask for offer **#6159** or a FREE catalog of NavPress products.

NAVPRESS
BRINGING TRUTH TO LIFE
www.navpress.com

Prices subject to change.